REBELLION TO RIOT

REBELLION TO RIOT

THE JAMAICAN CHURCH
IN NATION BUILDING

Devon Dick

Ian Randle Publishers

Kingston

First published, 2002 by
Ian Randle Publishers
11 Cunningham Avenue
Box 686
Kingston 6
Website: www.ianrandlepublishers.com

Reprinted 2003 by Ian Randle Publishers

ISBN 976-637-088-5 paperback

A catalogue record of this book is available from the National Library of
Jamaica.

Cover photo, *Rebellion at Roehamton Estate, St. James*, courtesy of the
National Library of Jamaica

Cover and book design by Michael Brooks

CONTENTS

LIST OF FIGURES

LIST OF TABLES

FOREWORD

Reverend Devon Dick sets out to show, and succeeds in showing, that the Church has been a leader in nation building in Jamaica since 1865. He documents, in a clear and concise manner, the contributions that the Jamaican Church has made to the building of the Jamaican nation through:

- Engagement at the grassroots of the society
- Leadership involvement in the formation of free villages and in community development
- The establishment of the primary and secondary school systems as well as the establishment of independent schools
- Breaching the colonial political structures by having ex-slaves buy land in quantities that made them have access to the vote
- Economic empowerment through various initiatives including skills training.

Reverend Devon Dick does not pretend to be neutral in his advocacy concerning the contribution of the Church. Rather, he explicitly sets out to counter the claim that the Jamaican Church has only been concerned with saving souls, putting up church buildings and offering heaven as the panacea for the earthly problems confronted by its members and the society at large. He goes further by confessing to the main sin of the Church which, in his view, is that of leading clergy members sometimes attempting to put distance between the church and mass protest action instigated and executed by church members.

Reverend Devon Dick sees the way forward in nation building as equitable land distribution, ecumenical cooperation by the several denominations (especially at the community level), engagement in the political arena with respect to critical issues facing the Jamaican society and a crusade on values and attitiudes.

If many would speak of the moral decay and barbarity displayed in some areas of Jamaican life, Reverend Dick leaves for discussion the complex question of what would have been the state of Jamaican society had the Church not been a leader in nation building over the last 160 years.

The appendices of Rebellion to Riot are highly informative because of their detailed documentation of the congregations listed by the Registrar of Companies and the dates of their registration; the denominations incorporated by acts of parliament, the list of Roman Catholic training centres, the list of the Jamaica Baptist Union medical and dental clinics and the distribution of church buildings by denominations. The appendices, by themselves, justify the addition of Rebellion to Riot to all public and personal libraries.

Professor Errol Miller
Head of the Faculty of Arts and Education
The University of the West Indies

PREFACE

On Sunday April 19, 1999, Boulevard Baptist Church, in association with congregations of the Mead-Haven Ministers Fraternal, hosted an evangelistic meeting in 100 Lane off Red Hills Road, St Andrew. This small 'horseshoe'-like lane of 120 metres with a population of about 400 was selected for an evangelistic outreach because warring political and drug gangs had fractured the community. Prior to this mass evangelistic effort, some Christians had been making regular visits to 100 Lane, Park Lane and Donmair Close or 'Black Ants' Lane with the express aim of making a difference in these communities. It was thought appropriate to have this crusade for building a better community during the Easter season when people would remember the resurrection of Jesus Christ and the new life and hope that He brings to people and communities. From all appearances the evangelistic effort was a success with a popular gospel band on stage playing contemporary religious music and the residents responding with lusty singing, hand clapping and dancing. Behind the stage little children were playing, oblivious to ministrations that were occurring a few metres away, while the evangelistic service reached a climax with a sermon delivered by Sydney Henry, an employee of Food for the Poor and member of Barbican Baptist. This young preacher, using 'rootsy' language and relevant illustrations, pointed the audience to a new life in Jesus Christ. Many responded with shouts of 'Amen' and 'Hallelujah' and it was not surprising when several residents came forward for prayer and made a commitment to Christ. During the service, a member of the prominent Mahfood family of Food for the Poor, who had been mingling and drinking beer with residents, pledged to build houses for the poorest members of the community. Christians left the meeting feeling that the wholistic needs of the residents had been addressed and a new day was dawning for the Church's involvement in a volatile area.

But at dawn, the people of 100 Lane and the surrounding communities staged a massive protest on Red Hills Road, which was part of an islandwide protest featuring roadblocks, burning of tyres and looting of businesses. It is at this point, April 20, 1999 - the date of the riot against the increase in gasoline prices as announced by the government -, that this book, *Rebellion to Riot: the Jamaican Church In Nation Building*, closes its analysis.

In the aftermath of the April Riot, Prime Minister P. J. Patterson invited Church leaders to Jamaica House to discuss the way forward and I was part of the delegation led by then President of the Jamaica Baptist Union, Reverend Jeffrey McKenzie. In an atmosphere of cordiality and candidness, the leaders held dialogue with the Prime Minister, wherein the country's problems were outlined and solutions offered. Subsequently, Church leaders met among themselves and Reverend Dr Burchell Taylor of Bethel Baptist, Dr Peter Morgan of Covenant Community and I presented papers on how the Church should respond to the April Riot. It was decided that there needed to be a seminar with community and national leaders, and the meeting was tentatively set for October 1999 at the Jamaica Conference Centre. However, in the hustle and bustle of life the meeting dropped off the agenda and became unfinished business.

Subsequently, Garfield Grandison, then Managing Editor of the Gleaner Company, persuaded me to write an article outlining the Church's contribution to Jamaica in the twentieth century. This was published in *The Gleaner* on December 27 and 28, 1999. There was an overwhelmingly positive response to my article, 'The Church in this Century', and I was duly encouraged to expand the work. This is it: my book which outlines and analyses the Church's contribution to nation building from 1865 to 1999. I undertook this project also with the aim of offering practical suggestions for the way forward and with the hope that the recommendations would be debated so that Jamaica might have a better tomorrow.

Professor George Beckford in *Persistent Poverty* analysed the persistent poverty in plantation economies of the world and offered a paradigm with a different philosophical spin. He states that 'what we need most are studies pregnant with ideas, not studies full of sterile detail. Ideas are what help people to understand problems and to pursue further inquiry.' This work is being offered in that spirit. Let the debate continue as we work to build a better nation.

ACKNOWLEDGEMENTS

This work on the role of the Jamaican Church in nation building between 1865 and 1999 would have been difficult to complete without the support and advice of the Chairman and Managing Director of the Gleaner Company, the Hon Oliver Clarke, and the helpful staff at the Gleaner library and the National Library. This work relies heavily on *The Gleaner*, the newspaper that has been writing the history of Jamaica since 1834, and from information gathered through interviews. In addition, I benefited from persons who commented on specific chapters including Oliver Clarke, Reverend Cawley Bolt of the United Theological College of the West Indies, Professors Patrick Bryan and Errol Miller of the University of the West Indies and former Secretary General of the Jamaica Teachers Association, Eric Downie. The critical pen of former Editor-in-Chief of *The Gleaner*, Wyvolyn Gager, and present Editor-in-Chief, Garfield Grandison, provided great editorial assistance. The critical eye of Lesley-Gail Atkinson, archaeologist of Jamaica National Heritage Trust, ensured the maintenance of historical integrity. The Boulevard Baptist church staff of Maud Daley, Dawn Largie, Heather Lloyd and Jean Treasure was crucial in making numerous contacts. The promptings of my children Deon, Duvaughn and Dana-Marie, who kept asking if I was still writing the book, were motivation to complete it. My wife, Mary, was general supervisor of the project. I am deeply indebted to the many persons who granted me interviews and the two denominations who responded to my letters seeking information. There are others, who inspired a thought or made a passing comment, who are too numerous to mention but still are necessary to acknowledge. They must accept full responsibility for the improvement of the final text over the first draft. Thanks to the Gleaner Company, Gordon's Equipment, National Housing Trust, J. H. Dunstan & Associates, Watts Investments, Jamaica Broilers Group Ltd., Ian K Agencies and the Bank of Nova Scotia which agreed to help underwrite the cost of publishing the book. Thanks also to the National Water Commission, Jentech, Paymasters, United General Insurance, Cari-Med Ltd., Pan Caribbean Merchant Bank, Blue Cross of Jamaica and the National Housing Development Corporation which made financial donations. Thanks also to those who had enough confidence in the book to engage in its pre-purchase - Boulevard Baptist Church, Jamaica National Building Society and Grace Kennedy Foundation. Truly, this was a team effort.

INTRODUCTION

A race had been freed but a nation had not been formed. (Lord Harris, Governor of Trinidad and Tobago, 1838)

Figure 1: Emancipation, August 1, 1838, Spanish Town Square
(Source: *Courtesy of the National Library of Jamaica*)

The Act of Emancipation granting 'full free' in 1838 meant that, legally, approximately 320,000 black slaves in Jamaica had been made free people. However, no thought was given to where the largest population of ex-slaves in the British West Indies would live. No community was prepared for them, no government was established that was inclusive of their racial group or responsive to their needs and no social amenities were provided for health care, recreation or education (except for a small educational grant). The primary concern of the British government was how the planters would survive, having lost the commodity of free labour. For this loss, the former slave-owners were handsomely compensated to the tune of £20,000,000. However, Henry George Grey, son of Prime Minister Earl

Grey, did suggest that the slaves ought to receive some money from the government as well, but he was scoffed at and the needs of the Blacks went unattended.

The lack of available socio-economic and political structure available to Blacks led to an extreme disparity in wealth distribution; the minority domination of political institutions; and to the control of arable lands by the upper classes. This ensured that the terms of employment of black workers was still determined by white employers. Blacks were, therefore, not free in the true sense of the word - they had little or no money; no home; no citizenship and they lived in a land where there was no cohesive nation state structure that cared for the wider community. The Blacks viewed Jamaica as a plantation from which to escape while the Whites saw Britain as home - viewing Jamaica as a temporary place of exile where they could get rich. It is within this context that the Jamaican Church, which was the main institution in closest contact with both the Blacks and the Whites, filled a void in developing a community and building a nation.

Rebellion to Riot: The Jamaican Church In Nation Building looks at the how the Jamaican Church has made an impact on society. It should be understood that the Jamaican Church, as stated here, refers to the collective Christian presence in society. It encompasses each individual Christian, as well as the clergy, congregations, spokesmen of denominations and national bodies that represent the Church. A congregation is a body of people who regularly assemble for religious services in a particular location, while a denomination is made up of like-minded congregations who share an administrative structure and are accountable to each other. The Church, in this context, can be thought of as a group of people who belong to an organisation that reflects the teachings, faith and practice of Jesus Christ whether as a body of congregants or a group of congregations, or a group of denominations. The Jamaican Church cannot, therefore, be restricted to the Jamaica Council of Churches, the Jamaica Association of Evangelicals, or the Jamaica Pentecostal Union, though they are part of it, and can speak on behalf of it. Rather, it is the collective Christian presence of which accredited persons can legitimately speak on its behalf. At times, the Jamaican Church is a reference to a Christian who speaks or acts as a representative of the Church, while at other times it may refer to the head of a denomination or a spokesperson for a council of denominations or a congregation. This is consistent with the Biblical understanding of Church where the 'Church' can be used in three different ways. It can mean the universal Church to which all Christians worldwide belong, as indicated in 1 Corinthians 12: 28, 'In the Church,

God has appointed first apostles....' It can mean a particular local Church in a specific place, 'the Church of God in Corinth....' (1Corinthians 1: 2) or it can also mean the actual assembly of Christians in any place, met together for worship, 'When you come together as a Church, there are divisions among you' (1 Corinthians 11: 18).

Just as there are various interpretations of who or what constitutes 'the Church', there are also various views of how the Jamaican Church should relate to the nation. There is the view that there should be separation of Church and State because they have two different agendas and, like oil and water, they cannot mix. The Church should not get involved in the affairs of the State or be beneficiaries of the State apparatus.

A second view is that the only relationship that the Church should have with society is to evangelise it, because the solution to the nation's problems is to be found in hosting continual crusades, 'Therefore go into all the world and make disciples of all nations....' (Matthew 28: 19). A third deterministic or fatalistic view claims that the Church cannot change anything because the biblical prophecies that God has ordained must be fulfilled. He will remedy the injustices, unaided, and in his own time (Exodus 14:13 and Matthew 24:6). There is yet another view that the Church is far superior to the State, and that the wider society cannot be expected to understand and follow the demands of the Christian faith. The strict and ideal values of the Church cannot be followed by the society but should be restricted to the membership of the faithful.

However, there is the final and preferred view that the Church should be in solidarity with the nation and, therefore, must be involved with the State. It is located in society and there ought to be a relationship between both, with the Church transforming the nation without 'being conformed to the world', (Romans 12: 2). Part of the ministry of the Church to the nation, as outlined in Matthew 25: 31-34, is to feed its people, quench their thirst, clothe and shelter them and visit them when they are sick and imprisoned. The Church as it ministers must do so within the context that the Church, as keeper of the society, must also help build the nation.

Many opportunities arose during this period for the Church to express solidarity with the people and function as nation builders, including the 1865 Morant Bay Rebellion, the 1938 Labour Riots, the Independence Movement of 1962, Walter Rodney Riots of 1968 and the Gas Riots of 1979, 1985, and 1999.

As evident, rebellions and riots have punctuated the prose of Jamaica's history and some have led to the development of the nation. Riots are confined to a small area and often with the intention of registering grave dissatisfaction, while rebellions are of a larger scale, characterised by armed resistance and the intent to overthrow a government or a system. Nevertheless, the distinction between rebellion and riot in the story of Jamaica is not clear cut and, in fact, the term rebellion is a misnomer and a reflection of colonial prejudice as in the case of both the Morant Bay Rebellion of 1865 and the Christmas Rebellion of 1831. For instance, the 1831 'rebellion' started as a passive resistance, while the 1865 'rebellion' was a protest march against injustices with no intention to overthrow a government. These protests were the oppressed people's main means of calling attention to deplorable conditions and for highlighting the hardships they were experiencing. Following these protests, the Jamaican Church became re-energised, pushing for the betterment of the people and society by instituting programmes for the progress of the nation, while the governing authorities became more responsive to the needs of the populace.

Figure 2: *Colour for Colour, Skin for Skin*
depicting The Morant Bay Rebellion
(Source: *Courtesy of Clinton Hutton*)

Rebellions and riots have been used throughout the history of Jamaica to make a statement and to stop misgovernance and it would therefore be dishonest to deny the value those rebellions and riots have played in the advancement of the country. The 1831 Rebellion moved the emancipation agenda forward, hastening the passing of the Emancipation Act in 1833 and it is obvious that the events of 1831 were beneficial to Jamaica and indeed the British West Indies.

It is a noteworthy accomplishment that Paul Bogle's Morant Bay Rebellion of 1865 led to the establishment of a more responsive and responsible government by the British. The year 1865 marked the beginning of the end of the British Empire, which was based on the supremacy of the British over the conquered races. It also marked the first time the British established systems for nation building, namely a civil service; a police force; an improved judicial system; an islandwide medical service; a Government Savings Bank; increased expenditure on education; the establishment of the Institute of Jamaica; an improved road network; cable communication with Europe and new irrigation schemes.

Both "rebellions" were protest movements in which leaders and members of the Church became involved in planning and executing manoeuvres which led to improvement in the quality of life for the Blacks. *Rebellion to Riot* relates the story of the struggle of Jamaica to move from being a collection of plantation societies, unfairly governed, to a nation of people working together through a shared administrative structure for prosperity. The chronicle begins with the Morant Bay Rebellion in 1865 - a year marked by unfair taxation of the poor; lack of educational opportunities for Blacks; insufficient medical facilities; lack of arable land; inadequate and irregularly paid wages and a biased judicial system.

The chronicle ends in 1999, when the Jamaican economy and society reached the end of a decade that had experienced considerable restructuring and realignment. The structural adjustment of the economy, which was formally initiated in 1983, continued into the 1990s and the economy was liberalised with foreign currency controls removed on September 25, 1991. This enabled businesses and individuals to legally hold foreign currency. In spite of liberalization, rapid inflation, reduced consumption and higher levels of poverty distinguished the first years of the decade. There were increases in welfare to the most vulnerable in the society and by 1994 there was evidence of recovery, which continued unevenly into the rest of the decade. There were many opportunities for the deepening of participation and consultations between the governed and the leaders. In fact, just months before the increases in taxes on gasoline in 1999, there was a consultation among the business leaders and the government officials at the Jamaica Conference Centre at which there was consensus about the need to increase taxes from gasoline sales. Nevertheless, persons felt alienated and, because a clear vision of the way forward was not shared with them, they banded together in protest in the April Gas riot of 1999.

Figure 3: April 1999 Gas Riot
(Source: *Courtesy of the Gleaner Company*)

The period between 1865 and 1999 can be described as a struggle against 'persistent poverty' in the midst of uneven improvements in social conditions, political rights and spiritual maturity. Although there were differences between the years 1865 and 1999 in societal structure, rights and governance, there were fundamental similarities because the governed, who often felt oppressed economically, consistently cried for justice and longed for positive future changes.

The Jamaican Church has been a silent doer with a low profile and she has not sought fanfare before or after the work was done. During the celebrations to mark Jamaica's independence in 1962, there was a float parade and the Church's float was at the back, which is symbolic of her working in the background in the cause of nation building and perhaps the reflection of a society that considers the Church as an afterthought. Nevertheless, there have been myriad ways in which the Church has significantly contributed to national development and this book is an attempt to record that history.

This book tells the story about how rebellions and riots have been used as a wake-up call against bad governance and how the Church has engaged in institutional development of a people frequently using the occasion of rebellions and riots as a catalyst for reflection, analysis and action. Chapter One outlines the growth of the Church, while chapter Two demonstrates that in economic empowerment, the Church was the first and foremost institution in providing economic development for the vast majority of Jamaicans. Chapter Three shows that it is the Church and not the State apparatus, that was the significant organisation in educating the people while Chapter Four posits that the Church had no equal in promoting proper and wholesome values through evangelism. Chapter Five discusses how the Church was the first institution that mobilised the people so their voices could be heard, political rights gained and representatives sent to the political forum. Chapter Six examines the weaknesses of the Church while Chapter Seven makes some recommendations as to the way forward.

CHAPTER ONE

THE EXPANDING CHURCH

Jamaica has the most churches per square mile in the world. (Oral tradition)

The Church was brought to the shores of Jamaica with the arrival, in 1494, of Christopher Columbus and his crew which included a chaplain of the Order of Mercy. Although it was a Christian crew, they showed no tolerance of the beliefs and believers of the Taino tribe and by 1665, the Tainos, the indigenous inhabitants of Jamaica, were completely wiped out along with their religion. The Africans, who replaced the Tainos in the seventeenth century as the primary labour force, were forced to repress their expressions of faith and so Christianity became the dominant religion. The dominance of Christianity was achieved through the importation of missionaries, mainly from Europe, which included Anglicans (1662), Moravians (1754), Baptists (1783), Methodists (1789), the Church of Scotland and the United Presbyterian (1814), the Church of Christ in Jamaica (1858), the Congregational Union (1876), the Society of Friends (1882), the Salvation Army (1887) and the Seventh-Day Adventists (1894). It was in the twentieth century, subsequent to the Depression of 1929 in America, however, that there was the greatest expansion of denominations with 547 being registered in the 1900s - the majority being Pentecostals or Church of God (See Figure 4 and Appendix I). These American-based groups gave great comfort to the lower socio-economic classes.

Each decade witnessed a steady growth in the number of denominations registered: 92 in the 1970s, 169 in the 1980s and 286 in the 1990s (See Figure 4). Additionally, in each of those three decades, an Act of Parliament incorporated 11 new denominations. In 1865, there were fewer than ten denominations in the island, but by 1999 there were 606 denominations (See Figure 5). This whopping increase of 6,060 per cent over 134 years indicates that the Church was on a growth spurt.

According to the list of churches, as recorded by the Registrar of Companies in 2001, there were 547 organisations that represented congregations or groups of congregations in 1999 (See Appendix I) and

1

another 59 denominations were incorporated by an Act of Parliament (See Appendix II). It is the older and well-established denominations that become legalised by an Act of Parliament, while the newer denominations prefer to register as a company, which takes a shorter time and is a simpler process. This enables them to meet the legal requirements of government to conduct business transactions and to obtain tax reduction benefits. Some of the 547 organisations that have been registered are not groups of congregations, but are individual congregations and ministries, which means that the growth of denominations might not be matched by a large membership and that there will be heads of congregations who will also be the head of the denomination because it is a single congregational unit. Nevertheless, there is a great number of congregations that could give rise to the belief that Jamaica has more churches per square mile than any other country. *The Guinness Book of World Records* does not record which country has the most churches per square mile; however, in the minds of most Jamaicans, Jamaica holds the record in this category.

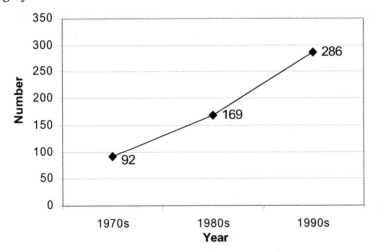

Figure 4: Growth of Registered Churches
(Source: *Registrar of Companies Church Listings 2001*)

Linstead, St Catherine, is an example of a town with a high concentration of congregations. The Social Development Commission (SDC) has designated six communities that belong to the Linstead zone. Table 1 shows the total number of church congregations in that zone and how these congregations are divided among the communities.

Community	Number of congregations
Linstead	20
Guy's Hill	23
Harewood	10
Redwood	9
Troja	5
Pear Tree Grove	1
Total	68
Average per community	**11.3**

Table 1: Congregations in the Linstead, St. Catherine Zone
(Source: *SDC Database on Church Listings 2001*)

A community is a group or groups of people who live in a defined geographic area who share common social amenities like churches, schools, post offices, community centres, libraries and have a sense of responsibility for each other's welfare. Based on Table 1, each community has an average of 11 congregations, and the Ministry of Local Government's statistics reveal that there were 692 communities as of 1999. Assuming that the average number of congregations per community in Linstead is representative of the number of congregations islandwide, it can be estimated that there are 7,843 congregations in Jamaica. Jamaica has 4,243 square miles, therefore, for every square mile a person travels, there will be 2 congregations. When you factor in a reduction of land space due to mountains, river courses, trees, forest, farmlands and agriculture, the concentration of congregations becomes higher.

According to J. Merle Davis, there were 1,200 congregations in Jamaica in 1942. Fifty-seven years later, there was a 553 per cent increase. In 1865, there were only 455 organisations -approximately 200 Anglican congregations, 130 Baptist congregations and 125 congregations comprising Roman Catholics, Church of Christ, Methodists, Presbyterians, Moravians and Native congregations. The growth in congregations between 1865-1999 has been phenomenal (See Figure 5). Interestingly, the Church is currently expanding numerically but unfortunately not at the same rate as the population as the gap widens significantly from 1960 and gets more pronounced afterwards (see Figure 6).

As the Jamaican Church continued to grow and expand from its germinal state in the mid-nineteenth century to its more mature state in the late twentieth century, its duties came to encompass activities for economic empowerment, educational development and political activism in addition to its initial role of saving souls.

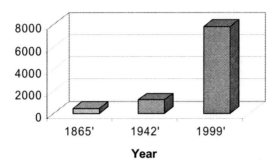

Figure 5: Growth of Congregations in Jamaica
(Source: *SDC Database on Church Listings 2001 and Davis 1942*)

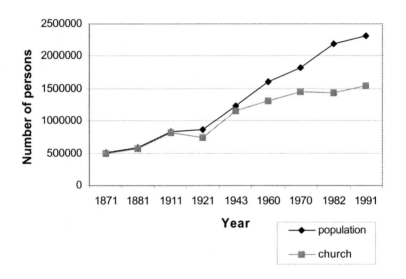

**Figure 6: A Comparison between Population Growth
& Church Affiliation Growth**
(Sources: *Demographic Statistics 2000 & Eighth Census of Jamaica
and its Dependencies 1943*)

Unfortunately, the outstanding contribution of the Church to nation building in the twentieth century was not been adequately recorded. The only attempt to analyse the contribution of the Church was carried out by British Methodist missionary, J. Merle Davis, in his book *The Church in the*

New Jamaica (1942). Davis tried to ascertain the major socio-economic problems of the island and the attitude of the Church towards them. He then made suggestions on how to deal with the problems. His conclusion was that the most serious problems of Jamaica were not economic, but rather social, cultural and spiritual:

> The sinister entail of slavery - as seen in illegitimacy, lack of responsibility, inertia, superstition, illiteracy and the absence of family life, which are among the chief enemies which stand in the path of Jamaica's progress - thwarts every effort toward economic development. (Ibid: 40)

The Church had her greatest expansion after 1942, yet nothing substantial was done to record this contribution to nation building and no analysis of that monumental activity was undertaken.

Countries	Number of persons emigrated
USA	46,000
Panama	45,000
Cuba	20,000
Other	35,000
Total	**146,000**

Table 2: Number of Persons who Emigrated between 1881-1921
(Source: *Sherlock & Bennett 1998:280*)

In addition, the contribution of the Church to the building of other nations has not been appreciated or recorded. The Church in Jamaica was not only a mission field but also a supplier of missionaries to other territories, especially between 1881 and 1921. As the people migrated (see Table 2), some took their Christian faith with them and established congregations in their adopted homelands. From 1901 to the 1960s, the Jamaican Church established missions in England, the United States of America, Nigeria, Zambia, Cameroons, Cayman Islands, Panama, Canada, Cuba and the Turks and Caicos. This led to notable achievements by some Jamaican clergy members, for instance, the Jamaican pastor, Reverend Hugh Sherlock, was awarded the Turks and Caicos Medal for outstanding service as a minister. In addition, the Jamaican Reverend Ephraim Alphonse translated the Bible into the language of the Valiente Indians of

Panama, while W. A. Thompson worked with Dr Miller to convert a translation of the Bible and Prayer Book into the Nupe language in 1906 in Nigeria. Around that time, Reverend Henry Ward, who spent twenty years in Nigeria, established the Hope Waddell Institute at Calabar, Nigeria for students who wished to acquire vocational skills at the tertiary level. Other Jamaicans who made outstanding contributions through the Church included L. A. Lennon from Mocho, Clarendon, who ascended the ranks of Nigerian nation builders, first as Canon of Lagos Cathedral (1929), then as Archdeacon of Ondo (1944) and finally as a member of the Legislative Council in Lagos, Nigeria. In 1908, missionaries Thomas Douglas and his wife, Herbert Simpson and his wife and Thomas McKay were commissioned by the Anglicans to teach in Nigeria. Douglas taught the people how to make sugar in the town of Zaria. In 1956, Canon John Hay was sent to the United Kingdom to integrate the congregations between the white with the black West Indian congregations in an effort to promote racial harmony.

In nation building there is need for economic empowerment, housing, education, moral values and opportunity to make decisions concerning one's welfare and as the Church expanded rapidly between 1865-1999 she was constantly and consistently involved in a significant way in all these facets of nation development.

**Figure 7: St James Cathedral, Spanish Town, the oldest
Anglican Cathedral outside of England**
(Source: *Courtesy of The Gleaner*)

CHAPTER TWO

ECONOMIC EMPOWERMENT

Give a man a fish, and you feed him for a day. Teach a man to fish, and you feed him for a lifetime. (Proverb)

Land was a symbol of freedom, thus it was not surprising that land was the major issue that led to the Morant Bay Rebellion 27 years after emancipation. The 'Rebellion' was due to the unwillingness of the planter class to accommodate peasant expansion and development. The Church movement, led by Paul Bogle, pastor of the Stony Gut chapel, agitated for land reform. The government belatedly responded in 1895 when, for the first time, it made land acquisition by the Blacks a policy. However, by 1910, when the policy was discontinued, 3,296 lots totalling 30,384 acres were distributed through 813 transactions (Sherlock & Bennett 1998: 206). That was miniscule compared to the 52,903 lots derived from the Free Village system started in 1838. It was therefore the Church, and not the State, which first distributed land to most people, through the partnership system of Free Villages.

The Jamaican Church could be said to have made it its duty to fulfil the African proverb 'It takes a village to raise a child' by implementing the Free Village system of land distribution which would satisfy the basic needs of the former slaves by providing them with land for shelter and farming. This was a necessary measure as the former slaves were frequently threatened with eviction from their dilapidated dwellings if they did not work on plantations for low wages and were prevented from utilising land on abandoned estates. Also, their ability to access Crown lands was restricted by artificially high prices.

To the chagrin of the planter class, the Church leaders, with assistance from overseas missionary bodies, began their Free Village system by acquiring large plots of land. They acted as financiers, sub-dividing the land into manageable lots and selling them inexpensively to the newly freed Blacks. These lots were surveyed, officially registered and titles were secured for each freeholder. They were residential with enough space for the owners to engage in crop cultivation. The size of the lots distributed was determined by the size of the family, with larger families getting the larger plots (which averaged four to five acres). The first such transaction occurred in June 1838, when ex-slave Henry Lunan, purchased the first lot of land from the Sligoville Free Village. This Free Village, founded by Reverend James Phillippo, was located in the hills behind Spanish Town, the then capital of Jamaica.

Figure 8: Free Village with Church House Sligoville, St. Catherine
(Source: *Courtesy of the National Library of Jamaica*)

The Villages were normally established in close proximity to the plantations. This allowed blacks access to employment, to their plots on the plantation and to their ancestors who were buried on the property of their former slave masters. Land ownership also gave them strong bargaining power when negotiating wages with their former owners because they had the option of supporting themselves from their own land rather than from the estates of their former owners. They were now the masters of their own destiny, giving their labour only when it suited them. Land ownership gave power to the people.

Each opening ceremony for a Free Village was marked by an address or sermon from a Church leader on social duties, personal responsibilities and the need for respect. Additionally, the Church continued to play an active role in Village life, adjudicating on disputes and petty offences. These villages were well planned and properly structured. Phillippo in *Jamaica its Past and Present State* gave a description of the layout of the Free Villages:

The villages were laid out in regular order, being divided into lots more or less intersected by roads or streets. The plots were usually in the form of an oblong square. The cottage was situated at an equal distance from each side of the allotments, and about eight or ten feet, more or less from the public thoroughfare (1969: 221).

Figure 9: Home Sweet Home
(Source: *Courtesy of the National Library of Jamaica*)

In these communities the Blacks lived in relative prosperity with the quality of their dwelling significantly improved from the dilapidated huts inhabited during slavery. Phillippo described peasant homes within a Free Village in positive terms.

They vary in size based on the number of members within the family. In general they were from 20 to 30 feet in length and from 14 to 16 feet in breadth. They were either neatly thatched, or shingled with pieces of hard wood hewn somewhat in the shape of slates. Some are built of stone or wood … being plastered also on the outside, and whitewashed. Many are ornamented with a portico in front to screen the sitting apartment from the sun and rain while for the admission of light and air, as well as to add to their appearance, all of them exhibit either shutters or jalousies, painted green or small glass windows (ibid).

9

The peasants were able to practice their distinctive cultural beliefs and bury their ancestors on their land according to their rites and rituals and to remember their customs in song and dance at times of marriages, births and changing of the seasons. They now had a farm, a family, a home, a heritage, peace, stability and hope. The Free Village system was a deliberate policy by the Church to create a community, provide shelter, alternative employment, food production, self-sufficiency, security of tenure for family stability and political rights for the oppressed blacks.

The Free Villages went on to become thriving communities, which have lasted well into the new millennium. Sligoville, Porus, Sturge Town, Bethany, Salem, Philadelphia, Wilberforce, Nazareth, Belle Castle and Kettering are among those which remain today. An important outcome of the Free Village was that it allowed blacks to demonstrate initiative, enterprise and co-operation in their ability to pool resources to purchase land.

Figure 10: Wattle and Daub House, Bushy Park, St Catherine
(Source: *Courtesy of the National Library of Jamaica*)

In his book *The West Indies: The Social and Religious Condition*, Edward Underhill underscored the importance of Free Villages to the Blacks and the nation as a whole when he noted that one half of the coffee and all of the pimento exported were from the produce of the peasantry (pp. 290-91). These farmers also cultivated sugar cane, bananas, ginger and logwood for the domestic and export markets, with export production from the peasantry doubling by 1890 and an adequate supply of food being made available for local consumption for the first time.

Sherlock and Bennett also credited the system of free-holdings by the Blacks with the introduction of the banana trade to Jamaica, 'The Black peasant pioneered the Jamaica banana trade and in so doing also contributed to the development of the Jamaica tourist industry' (p. 277). The Jamaican peasantry aided the economy by diversifying the range of export crops when King Sugar's reign was waning. In 1938, bananas accounted for 59 per cent of the Jamaican exports, while sugar accounted for 18 per cent. The 'arrival' of banana prompted a social revolution, whereby this versatile staple became an important part of the local cuisine, making its way to the breakfast, lunch and dinner tables. The man who cultivated bananas became an icon of strength and resilience to the Jamaican people and was immortalized by Evan Jones in his poem, *The Song of the Banana Man*. The banana also provided the opportunity for a local scientific breakthrough when the popular Gross Michel variety was decimated by disease and J. B. Sutherland developed the handier, more resistant Lacatan variety.

Building Societies

Another Jamaican institution that could be considered attributable to the Church was the 'building society': so called because it provided a scheme for home-ownership which served to 'build' the society. Home ownership was a foundational block in the formation of a sustainable society and the founding of building societies was a gigantic leap toward assisting working and middle-class people to realize their dream of home-ownership. The Reverend W. G. Gardner founded the first building society, Kingston Benefit Building Society, in 1834, in the growing city of Kingston. Reverend Henry Clarke in Westmoreland followed suit after bemoaning, 'The great need of this parish ever since I came to it has been houses, and I have long prayed to the Lord to send us help in this matter' (James Walvin, *The Life and Times of Henry Clarke* p. 52). His prayers were answered by the birth of the Westmoreland Building Society in 1874 - a forerunner of the Jamaica National Building Society (JNBS). The JNBS, currently the largest building society in Jamaica, was a result of a series of mergers including the St Ann Building Society, which was founded in 1874 by Reverend Josias Cork, and the St Mary Building Society, which

11

was founded in 1915 by the Reverend Edwin Touzalin. In 1878, the Reverend E. W. Downer, rector of the Kingston Parish Church, inspired members of his congregation to pool their savings in order to own land - an action that gave birth to the Victoria Mutual Building Society, whose aim was to meet the needs of those who wanted to own a home. These Church-initiated building societies rank among the largest indigenous businesses in the island and they continue to facilitate home-ownership for thousands of Jamaicans (See Table 3).

Figure 11: Jamaica National Building Society Headquarters
(Source: *Courtesy of the Jamaica National Building Society*)

Decades	Government	Building Societies	Private Sector
1960s	14,761	18,000*	Nil
1970s	25,632	13,621	7,074
1980s	19,046	16,777	7,604
1990s	40,140	24,242	18,657
Total	99,579	72,640	33,335

* Estimated

Table 3: Number of Housing Solutions 1960-99
(Source: *The Social and Economic Survey 1957-99*)

12

The building societies' figures do not include lands made available by individual congregations, nor do they include houses built for the indigent by the Church. So the hundreds who would have benefited from lands made available through community developments such as Farm Heights, St James in the 1970s, and Calabar lands, St Andrew, in the 1980s and 1990s would not have been included. The government figures, however, include houses erected for the indigent and squatter upgrading.

The purchase of a house is usually the largest investment a person can make as it provides security for the family and serves as an important means of collateral for embarking on other investments. The acquisition of a house and land is central to attaining economic empowerment and creating financial security. Through its programme of the Free Village and the establishment of building societies, the Church has made a significant contribution to nation building.

Credit Unions

In 1938, on the one hundredth anniversary of the abolition of slavery, the Frome Riots took place. The sugar workers in Westmoreland protested against the treatment they experienced under the British-owned Sugar Company, Tate and Lyle. The employers were dictatorial, the wages were low, the housing inadequate and during 'crop time' the workers toiled seven days a week for a mere nine pence a day. To add insult to injury, they were laid off during the 'off season' for months without any compensation while the managers continued to enjoy an opulent lifestyle year-round. A dispute with wage clerks flared into a violent strike in April 1938 and on May 3, 1938, cane fields were set afire and a riot ensued. Four workers were killed, 13 wounded and more than 100 were arrested during efforts to quash the riot. There was also the Waterfront Strike by dockworkers, which prevented the export and import of goods. The Frome Riots, along with the Waterfront Strike by dockworkers constituted a national crisis, which elicited a response from the Church to alleviate the plight of the workers. After the Labour Riots, a commission was established to investigate the social conditions that led to the unrest of the 1930s. In an attempt to alleviate the harsh social conditions, the Church started the credit union movement.

In January 1942, the Church responded by forming the Sodality Credit Union to ensure financial security for workers, and provide a source from which they might borrow money at a low rate of interest. At that time, the usurers had a stranglehold on the working classes who laboured on the estates and wharves, charging them exorbitant rates of up to 1000 per cent interest per annum. Father John Peter Sullivan was given a special mandate by the Roman Catholics to set up an organisation that would lend money at a lower rate of interest. He subsequently established the Jamaica Cooperative Credit Union League in July 1942 to co-ordinate the work of all the credit unions. By 1944, the Roman Catholics had 178 Credit Union Study Groups and Saving Unions in Jamaica and their activities were extended to 20 other Caribbean territories.

Figure 12: Frome Sugar Estate - Westmoreland
(Source: *Courtesy of the National Library of Jamaica*)

In 1971, Reverend Oswald Thorbourne founded the Churches Cooperative Credit Union, an amalgamation of the Kingston Moravian, All Saints Anglican and Lyndhurst Methodist congregations. The name 'Churches' was used because the leaders wanted it to be representative of all its members and they wanted to attract more members from the Church community from which they could legally recruit. It started with a membership of 853 persons and a share capital of $80,000 and has since grown to a membership of approximately 60,000 with an asset base of J$1billion. Following on the heels of the success of the Churches Credit Union was the establishment of the St Elizabeth Cooperative Credit Union in 1972, another flourishing financial institution, also marshalled by

Oswald Thorbourne.

By 1999, there were 65 credit unions with an aggregate membership of 572,074 and share capital and deposits of J$12 billion. The strength of the movement is evident from the fact that it, like building societies, survived the fallout in the financial sector from 1996-98. In that difficult economic climate, it was the credit unions that had the biggest percentage increase in assets (See Table 4).

Institution	Assets in 1995 (J$B)	Assets in 1999 (J$B)	Percentage (%) increase
Banks	121	192	58.7
Credit Unions	4	12	200
Merchant Banks	17	10	41
Finance Houses	6	7	16.7

Table 4: Assets of Financial Institutions
(Source: *The Social and Economic Survey 1957-99*)

Credit unions have grown to play a role in the financial sector and with a high growth trend, they are poised to play a more significant role in the development of the nation through their prudent investments, low interest rates on the reducing balance and small dividends on shares. The reliance of credit unions on prayer and divine guidance must not be underestimated. This seems to have helped them through the financial sector meltdown and even allowed them to gain strength.

The credit union, the small man's bank, is owned and managed by all its members who have a say in electing leaders of the organisation. They also operate profitably although profit maximization was not the main preoccupation.

Because of the strength, vision and mission of the credit union movement, many ordinary Jamaicans own their own homes, furniture, appliances, businesses and motor vehicles and experience social mobility through higher education, funded by borrowings.

Christian Benevolence: Reaching out to People

Persons living in poverty find it difficult to provide the minimum requirements for their existence and, as such, are prevented from leading a life of dignity. In order to assist those who are most vulnerable, the Church developed programmes in the areas of:

Health - providing clinics, medical supplies, pharmacies, hygiene training, nutrition, access to potable water and communal washrooms and bathrooms.

Agriculture - establishing agro-industries, livestock and goat rearing, chicken and fish farms, forestry planting and protection, pepper and coffee planting.

Micro-industries - teaching handcraft, designing and dressmaking, small trade, small business, printing, cottage industries and food processing such as a banana chips factory and Implementing recycling plastic projects and providing tools and equipment.

Transportation - providing public transportation via buses or motor vehicles and the transportation of goods and rehabilitating roads.

Housing - providing of low cost houses and places of safety and short-term residence.

These initiatives have gone a long way in alleviating poverty and aiding those in need while affirming their human dignity. From the inception of theological training in Jamaica in 1843, the importance of agriculture was understood. Not only was it compulsory for pastors to undertake a course in agriculture, but the Church owned vast acres of land which it has put to good use - growing crops and processing them for marketing. In the 1990s, the Church farmed coffee in James Hill, Clarendon, and in 1983, in Maldon, St James, it became involved in banana chip production. In Mandeville, it set up Westico Foods, a bakery that produces quality cereals and baked products. In addition to its agricultural contribution, the Church (1998-1999) organised the repair of roads using funding from the Jamaica Social Investment Fund.

Figure 13: St Matthew's Anglican Church Pastry Shop
(Courtesy of the Gleaner Company)

Although congregations initially executed their benevolence pro-gramme individually, there came a time when a collaborative effort became necessary to take strong social action and make a greater impact. The social and economic unrest of the 1938 Labour Riots precipitated the Church's response and resulted in the formation of the Jamaica Christian Council in 1941 which was comprised of the ten principal denominations - the Anglicans, the Jamaica Baptist Union, the Presbyterians, the Congre-gationalists, the Methodists, the Moravians, the Disciples of Christ, the Church of God, the Salvation Army and the Religious Society of Friends. The Jamaica Christian Council became the agency through which the Church began to express solidarity with persons who were destitute by pooling their financial and human resources for social action.

Figure 14: Mount Olivet Church and School
(Source: *Courtesy of the National Library of Jamaica*)

In addition, the Church established shelters for the destitute, places of safety for the vulnerable, Day Care Centres for babies, Night Shelters, Remand Homes and Transient Homes. Food For The Poor, a Christian aid organisation, has built 1,200 houses between 1982-99 for destitute fam-ilies and persons with severe handicaps.

Children's Homes

Communal homes for the young were also built. These children's homes provided care and protection for those children who were orphaned, abandoned, destitute, rescued from abusive situations and who thus become wards of the State. The children are raised in a big family setting in which they develop bonds and learn lessons of self esteem. Respect for self and others is reinforced and domestic chores are also allocated based on ability to manage. Worship is an important part of these home and spiritual values are taught through bible reading, prayer, singing, dancing, teaching and preaching. Opportunities to obtain formal education are provided and field trips to places of national significance are co-ordinated to help them become culturally aware and develop their national identity. After school, time is also allocated for homework and in some homes, time is scheduled for the acquisition of skills like woodworking, cookery and dressmaking. These activities are designed to equip the children with skills that will eventually allow them to generate income and support themselves, hone their leadership qualities and prepare them to be good citizens. Many of the children who have graduated from these homes have become teachers, nurses, pilots, dressmakers and business people. A typical home would be staffed with a matron, nurse, teachers, domestics and a guard. The nurse would provide basic medical and first aid services and if there is need for other medical, dental and optical services then outside professionals would provide these services to the residents of the homes. Table 5 lists the Children's Homes that were established by the Church. Seventy five per cent of the licensed Children's Homes in Jamaica are owned and operated by the Church. So impressive has been the work of the Church among the needy and deprived that, in 1999, the government asked the Church to manage the few remaining public owned places of safety.

Centres and Programmes for the Physically and Mentally Challenged

The Church established various centres to provide assistance for the physically and mentally challenged (See Table 6), affirming persons with disabilities as persons with other abilities. In this way the Church has tangibly demonstrated its concern by offering hope and enabling the participants to acquire literacy and other occupational skills including woodwork, computing and home economics. In addition, the Church has conducted special worship services for the hearing impaired at various locations island-wide.

Centre	Parish	Date of Establishment
Belmont Orphanage	Westmoreland	1892
The Nest	St Andrew	1904
The Wortley Home for Girls	St Andrew	1918
The Swift Purcell Home for Boys	St Mary	1919
The Pringle Home	St Mary	1921
The Garland Hall Memorial Home	St James	1922
Methodist Deaconess Home for Girls	St Andrew	1928
The New Broughton Home for Boys *	Manchester	1940
The St Monica's Home for Girls	Clarendon	1953
Jamaica Christian Boys' Home	St Andrew	1956
The Clifton's Boys' Home	Westmoreland	1958
St John's Bosco for Boys	Manchester	1960
The Mount Olivet Home for Boys	Manchester	1967
St Andrew Hostel for Girls	St Andrew	1969
Windsor Lodge	Manchester	1972
The National Children's Home	St Andrew	1973
The Elsie Bemand Home for Girls	St Ann	1979
New Beginnings Boys Home	Hanover	1986
Lyndale for Girls	St Mary	1992
Mary's Child	Kingston	1995
Home of Charlotte Children	St James	1998

* The New Broughton Home for Boys is now a place for old ex-convicts.

Table 5 : Children's Homes Established by the Church
(Source: *Children Services Division & Personal Communication*)

Furthermore, the Church hosts sign language classes so that members can better communicate with the hearing impaired and better understand their needs. It also launched the Association for the Care of the Deaf and Dumb in 1943, which was later renamed the Jamaica Association for the Deaf Ltd, an organisation that lobbies the government and the nation to be more sensitive to the needs of the hearing impaired. Lobbying also takes place on behalf of the physically challenged and, among other things, the programme has brought about improved access to church buildings and offices for persons with disabilities.

Centre	Challenge	Date of Establishment
The Salvation Army's School	Blind	1927
St Christopher's School	Deaf and Dumb	1943
The Lister Mair/Gilby	Deaf	1970
Maranatha School	Deaf	1976
Carberry Court Special School	General disability	1982
The Faith Centre	Retarded children and adults afflicted with Down's Syndrome	1985
McCam Child Development Centre	Special needs	1986
Liberty Preparatory	Autism	1996

Table 6: Centres for the Physically and Mentally Challenged
(Sources: *National Library of Jamaica and Personal Communication*)

Homes for the Aged

The Church has provided Homes for the Aged since 1883 (See Table 7). These Homes, which are usually either free or available for a minimal cost, offer occupational therapy for the total development of the residents who, though old, are not helpless. The Homes for the Aged ensure that the residents receive adequate medical care, regular well-balanced meals and opportunities for interaction.

Whereas Homes for the Aged cater mostly to the elderly who are well, Nursing Homes cater to the elderly who are usually ill. There are thirty-eight registered Nursing Homes in Jamaica and five are operated by the Church namely, Beulah Rest Home, Emmanuel Home for the Aged, Gallimore/MacPherson Home for Senior Citizens, Moravian Home for the Aged and United Church Senior Citizen's Home. The Church operates Nursing Homes that are not registered and so do not come under the jurisdiction of the Nursing Home Registration Act which is monitored by the Ministry of Health.

Centre	Date of Establishment
St. Matthew's Anglican Church	1883
Villa Maria for the Aged Women	1949
The Ozanam Home	1953
St. Andrew Parish Church Home	1956
The Farquharson Home for the aged clergy, widows and dependents	1956
Elizabeth Home for the Aged	1963
The Amy Muschett Home for the Aged	1963
The Bishop Gibson Home for the Aged	1963
The Horizon Home for Aged Women	1965
The St Clair Home for Aged Men	1970
Christian Brethren Home for the Aged	1972
The Faydene Home for the Aged	1972
Mother Russell Memorial Home for geriatric care	1979
The St. Monica's Home for the Aged and Infirm	1981

Table 7: Homes for the Aged Established by the Church
(Source: *Churches, Jamaica, National Library & Personal Communication*)

Shelters for the Destitute

There is a place for the homeless and the nomadic, who have been abandoned by their families or who have suffered great misfortune and they find rest and solace in homes for the destitute. The opening of shelters for the destitute is a recent ministry of the church that started in the 1970s (See Table 8). In these shelters attention was also given to the needs of the soul.

Centre	Target Group	Date of Establishment
The Sunset Rehabilitation Centre	For persons who have committed crimes and are allowed to go home at periodic intervals	1976
Jacob's Well	A place of shelter for destitute adults	1987
Good Shepherd	A home for homeless persons	1989
The Lord's Place	Houses persons of different ages and with various needs	1994
HIV/AIDS Hospice	Adults, children with HIV/AIDS	1997

Table 8: Shelters for the Destitute
(Source: *Gleaner Supplement March 22, 2000;*
Churches, Jamaica, The National Library)

Training Centres and Programmes for the Able-bodied

The Church was conscious of the needs of those with the handicap of poverty and addressed the issue of unemployment by creating various skills training centres across the island. In the 1970s, the economy underwent structural adjustment, which brought a decrease in spending, by the State, on social services. The Church tried to fill this gap by opening and operating more skills training centres, although it had been doing so from as early as the late nineteenth century (See Table 9). The Roman Catholic Church, for instance, operates 20 skills training centres (See Appendix III).

Many congregations also provide free legal aid and counselling services; run drug rehabilitation centres, thrift shops and provide help for persons with other needs. They also offer scholarships valuing $1 million annually to needy students. The Church also provides free, competent and confidential chaplaincy services for persons having emotional, mental and spiritual problems and who could not normally afford these services. The quality of the lives of the destitute has been lifted through the efforts of the Church.

Centre	Target Group/Function	Date of Establishment
Alpha Approved School	Training in various trades, craft and skills for orphans from broken homes	1892
Boys' Town	Teach persons career guidance & basic education	1940
Operation Friendship	Training in craft and community development	1958
Kelly Lawson Training Centre	Girls	1962
The Roper Centre	Counselling and training in handicrafts for discharged prisoners	1964
The Churches Advisory Bureau	Residents of Western Kingston	1967

Table 9: Centres for Training the Able-bodied
(Sources: *The National Library of Jamaica and Davis:1998*)

Para-Church Organisations

In the 1930s and the 1940s, the Church was the driving force behind many para-church organisations and movements, including:

- The YMCA (Young Men's Christian Association),
- The YWCA (Young Women's Christian Association),
- The SCM (Student Christian Movement)

These organisations gave thousands of youths, who were poor, an opportunity for development and a fair start in life. The idea of the Council of Voluntary Social Services (CVSS) came out of a Christian Auxiliary Movement (CAM) meeting in 1940 which identified the need for an umbrella organisation to co-ordinate the fragmented voluntary organisations so that the combined force would be better equipped and trained to fill the needs of the community. A member of CAM, Jessie Irwin, was asked by then Premier and now National Hero, Norman Manley, to establish the CVSS and, within two years, CVSS had a membership of 38 groups with most being church-related.

Another initiative of the Church was a National Ecumenical Church Loan Fund Committee, formed in November 1980, which provided soft loans for congregations and community development projects and programmes. Loans, not grants, were given as an instrument of development, without regard to religious, racial or political considerations. The beneficiaries, Christian groups and the rural poor, used the money appropriately and avoided dependency and external indebtedness. Access to financing has allowed those persons who are disadvantaged to grasp economic opportunities including capital formation and re-investing in small businesses. These ventures have enhanced self-esteem, given women economic independence, enhanced technical and business management skills and provided an opportunity for cooperatives.

Hospitals, Medical Centres and Burial Assistance

In 1865, there was no rural medical care and public health was neglected, so it was not surprising that in the 1860s cholera and smallpox epidemics claimed one tenth of the population. The Church was committed to the treatment of diseases through the establishment of hospitals and the operation of health clinics and it spared no effort in trying to rid the country of diseases that were endangering the lives of its citizens. It was recognised that a healthy worker was more productive and efficient. In 1908, a Nursing Hostel for the sick was set up on East Street. In the 1940s, the Church set up a leprosarium, which housed those afflicted with the dreaded disease of leprosy and helped to curb its pervasiveness in communities. The Church is currently a leading private healthcare provider and, like the government, is involved in the operations of four hospitals in the Corporate Area. The Church established the following hospitals:

- St Joseph's Hospital - opened by the Roman Catholics in 1911
- Nuttall - opened by the Anglicans in 1923
- Andrews Memorial - opened by the Seventh Day Adventists in 1944
- Medical Associates Hospital - partnered and partially funded by the Methodists in 1959.

The Baptists have also contributed greatly by establishing 19 medical clinics islandwide (See Appendix IV) and thousands continue to benefit from the Church's dental and health clinics all over the island. The Church is well known for her work in wholistic health care, which seeks to facilitate healing for the person in mind, body and spirit and improve social relationships through the promotion of primary health care and counselling services.

The Church ministers to persons both in life and in death. Andrew Mowatt, Methodist Circuit Steward (the highest non-clergy position in the Methodist Church), pioneered the Jamaica Burial Scheme in Banbury, Linstead, St Catherine, in 1901 to care for the sick, perform the last rites and assist in burials. The dues were reasonable with members contributing a penny a month to receive benefits after six months. In 1930 there were 133 branches with a membership of 25,000 and dependents of twice that number. By 1976, the number had increased to 155 branches.

Figure 15: St Joseph's Hospital, Kingston
(Source: *Courtesy of the Gleaner Company*)

Emergency Services

Jamaica, prone to natural disasters, has suffered from serious earthquakes and hurricanes, which have caused great hardships and have worsened poverty. The Church has always responded at such times of crisis with a large heart and a willing hand. Nineteen forty-four was the year of the cyclone that devastated St. Mary and Portland, and it was noticed with interest and justifiable pride, that the Church rendered good service in the most damaged areas. After hurricane Charlie in August 1951, the Church responded by engaging in giving cash and kind to help the most needy and again in 1979 when devastating rains washed away roads, houses and people. The Church again rallied to the aid of the people after Hurricane Gilbert in September 1988. This proved to be the first time that so many denominations were in one accord for social rehabilitation and the equitable distribution of relief under the agency of Project Accord. This cooperative group was formed at the initiative of then Prime Minister Edward Seaga and it was very successful in distributing relief supplies quickly and fairly with some 6,000 persons at the National Arena and thousands more across the island being fed daily. The Church also helped to rebuild many homes and communities, provided medical teams, clothing and other basic supplies, and provided seed money to start small businesses. In times of natural disaster, the Church is on call to mobilise assistance for those affected, especially the poor. The Church buildings are also often available for use as relief shelters for those displaced by disasters.

Crusades Against Gambling

The Church has consistently objected to gambling on the premise that people should work for a living and not take shortcuts, especially with games of chance that exploit those who can least afford it.

In the late 1960s and early 1970s, the Church was militant in her opposition of the lottery. Twenty-one denominations and Church bodies, of which the Jamaica Council of Churches was only one, expressed strong dissatisfaction (See Appendix V). The Church's opposition to the National Lottery remains the single most important issue on which the Church has vigorously protested. It is believed by some that the Church's opposition to the National Lottery cost the Jamaica Labour Party (JLP) the elections in 1972, however, the reliable Stone Poll of 1972 claims that the lottery issue was merely a sideshow that did not gain the People's National Party (PNP) any votes.

In the 1980s, the casino gambling issue saw the Church uniting to oppose its introduction and, again, this group was not confined to the Jamaica Council of Churches but included other Church bodies. The 1981 Carl Stone Poll found that 58 per cent of Jamaicans were against casino gambling while 32 per cent were for its introduction but by 1986 the respected pollster ascertained that 69 per cent of Jamaicans were against casino gambling while 22 per cent were for it. This increase in the opposition to casino gambling was due to the tremendous united national campaign, which effectively prevented the wholesale introduction of casino gambling.

The paradox is that the PNP government, which was so against the National Lottery in the early 1970s, has played a three-card trick by introducing three major gambling ventures while still maintaining an anti-casino line. The PNP government allowed the establishment of the Racing Pools, the placing of a maximum of 70 gambling machines per hotel and granted a licence to operate a lottery. The first lottery, which was called 'Scratch and Win', folded in 1992 due to unaudited losses of $25 million not to mention losses for the promoters and the government, who was owed millions of dollars and the biggest losers of all, the vast majority of players. No wonder the game was nicknamed, 'Scratch and Lose'. However, Howard Hamilton, the former Chairman of the defunct lottery, started the Jamaica Lottery Company in 1994, which flourished and saw people forming long queues to purchase tickets. Although, for most, the dreams have turned into a nightmare, the dreamers live on, ignoring the Church's boycott of the Bank of Nova Scotia and other businesses that sold lottery tickets. The gambling industry, during the 1990s, experienced great growth with 'One Armed Bandits', gambling machines, becoming prevalent in bars, games rooms and hotels as well as with electronic black jack, roulette machines and 'joker poker'. Interestingly, at least one government-owned hotel advertises, as one of its major attractions, a casino, even though the government officially has an anti casino stance.

To further compound the issue, the Roman Catholics are not against gambling, as long as it is carried out for recreational purposes and the player can afford it. They draw the line, however, if the gambling starts to harm the family unit. The Roman Catholics' relaxed stance on the issue was demonstrated prior to 1976 when Mass was celebrated in a room at the Caymanas Park racetrack, courtesy of Joseph Armond, a Roman Catholic. Additionally, problems were caused within the wider church community when Father Richard Albert, who founded St Patrick's Foundation, accepted a donation of J$30,000 from a lottery company in 1995. It took the protest of the Jamaica Council of Churches and the intervention of the Roman Catholic Bishop to reverse that action.

The perception of the Church seemingly condoning gambling occurred again in 1996 when the National Director of the 'Reggae Boyz' football team, Rene Simoes, regularly was seen wearing his trademark T-shirt, with the words 'Jesus Saves' boldly written on the back of his shirt while-sporting the logo of the Sports Development Foundation on the front. The Sports Development Foundation, which sponsored the football programme with millions of dollars, was funded by revenue collected from lottery sales.

Ironically, the Church has been accused of enriching itself rather than empowering people and of being self-serving rather than being concerned with helping the poor. The critics cite the tax benefits available to some congregations. For example in 1977, the denominations that were incorporated by Parliament were granted tax exemptions on items used in worship and, in the 1970s, the Income Tax Act was amended so that clergymen would not be required to pay taxes on housing allowance (which, incidentally, was revoked in the 1980s). Section 10 of the Property Tax Act was also amended to provide for a tax exemption for all Church-owned buildings - chapels, rectories, caretaker's cottages, school rooms or church halls - along with the lands immediately attached to them, provided that that area of land did not exceed one acre. There was a time when congregations were exempt from paying water bills, but that soon changed and they now pay a discounted rate.

The General Consumption Tax (GCT) Act states that churches are allowed exemption on goods of a non-consumable nature that are purchased or imported solely for furnishing or decorating a place of worship. Under that Act and, according to the 1995-99 record under 'Places of Worship' concession code 5000, the Church received tax exemptions valued at J\$10.52 million but this does not include the other exemptions that can be granted by ministerial order of the Minister of Finance, which valued J\$100 million in 1999. These exemptions were granted to cover taxes on cars, musical instruments, refrigerators, public address systems and other effects that facilitate worship. This is not a huge tax exemption when compared to other groups that receive tax exemptions like police officers, certain civil servants, parliamentarians, senators and custodes. In addition, the basic salary paid to clergy is quite low with some starting at \$24,000 a month and that is taxed. On the balance, the Church practises 'it is better to give than to receive'.

The Church facilitated economic empowerment of the people, who had their basic needs met through the acquisition of housing and each person was treated as an equal partner in the economic life of the community. Economic empowerment was further facilitated by the Church's involvement in caring for the most vulnerable through her role in health care and disaster relief, indeed the Church has sought to care for the old, infirm, physically challenged, minorities, outcasts and the unpopular.

CHAPTER THREE

EDUCATING THE FREED

If you think that education is expensive, try ignorance. (Derek Bok, former President of Harvard University, USA)

Education was essentially a religious matter in England and the jewel in her crown, Jamaica, during the post-emancipation era. The Church undertook that responsibility because education could then be used as a means of evangelism. It was claimed that persons were more receptive to the ministrations of the gospel when they had the ability to read and write. Education was also seen as a vehicle for social control in that it was believed that educated persons were less likely to revolt and would be more submissive and obedient to their masters as taught by some sections of the Holy Bible. These persons would also be more willing to accept their lot in life. The ruling class was especially comfortable with that role of education, which would reinforce class and colour divisions in which the whites ruled and the Blacks were their subjects. Education therefore socialised the Blacks to accept their place at the bottom of the social ladder and provided them with literacy, agricultural and industrial skills to prepare them only for vocational tasks. They, however, viewed education as a means of social mobility with the possibility of being able to rise to any position in society. The truth is that the Church saw education in all three roles as facilitating social mobility, while being a means of evangelism and social control.

During slavery there was little formal education for the Blacks, but after 1834 with the passing of the Emancipation Act, which freed all children six years and under, it meant children were now available for instruction. The core curriculum consisted of religious instruction plus reading the Bible but sometimes schools added other courses such as writing and arithmetic. The objectives of this meagre educational fare was the Christian conversion of the former slaves and making the Blacks acquiescent and docile to alleviate the threat of rebellion. After this initial activity the Church became more deeply involved in the educational enterprise. It went about the task of educating the freed with gusto, providing early-childhood education straight through to tertiary-level education.

Teacher Training

The Church founded teacher-training education in Jamaica, when the Moravians established a college in Refuge, Trelawny in 1832. Four years later, the Lady Mico Charity, a Christian charity, established Mico. The Church tried to alleviate the shortage of teachers by establishing teacher training facilities, as seen by the Moravians establishing Fairfield in 1839 and the Baptists operating a teacher-training component alongside the Calabar Theological College in 1843 at Rio Bueno, Trelawny. The Presbyterians established a college in Montego Bay which was eventually closed in 1877. In 1845, the government joined the foray in teacher training, but similar to Refuge that effort did not last long. After 1846, the recruitment of teachers from Britain declined as a result of the cessation of the Negro Education Grant. To counter this short fall, the teachers colleges operated by the Church took up the short fall and produced teachers for the classrooms; a job they did more cost effectively than all other colleges. By 1865, all the teacher training was being conducted by the Church as seen by the survival of Mico, Fairfield, Calabar, the one established in Montego Bay by the Presbyterians, and Bethlehem in St Elizabeth in 1861 under the auspices of the Moravians.

After the Morant Bay Rebellion and under the enlightened governorship of John Peter Grant a Government Training College was established, which lasted for 20 years. By 1885 the government also established Shortwood Teachers' College, St Andrew to train female teachers. In 1899, the government withdrew all financial help to Church colleges that trained males and so it was no surprise when Fairfield closed in 1899 and Calabar in 1890. St. Joseph's Teachers' College, St Andrew started in 1897 by the Roman Catholics survived because it was involved in training females. So at the beginning of the twentieth century, the institutional provision for teacher training were all church related, except for Shortwood. These institutional arrangements remained for 53 years until the Seventh Day Adventists opened a teacher training department at West Indies College in Manchester in 1943, and the government opened Moneague (1956) in St Ann; Sam Sharpe (1975) in St James, and Passley (1981) in Portland. The Church did not withdraw from erecting teachers' colleges during the heyday of the government's construction of teachers colleges (1956-1981) but erected Church's Teachers' College (1965) in Manchester via the Anglicans. In 1999, there were nine teachers' colleges, of which five were Chuch-related, namely:

* Mico
* Bethlehem

- Church's
- West Indies College
- St. Josephs

It is therefore true to say that during the period 1865-1999 the Church was the leading provider of teacher training. During the period 1872 to 1990 the number of elementary school teachers in the system moved from 508 in 1872 to 10,075 in 1990 (See Figure 16), which is a percentage increase of 504. This trend continued in the 1990s with the number of students enrolled moving from 3,590 in 1995 to 3,946 in 1999. This was great growth when it is recalled that the enrolment in teachers' college moved from 89 in 1870 to 154 in 1889. The Church would have been largely responsible for this phenomenal improvement in teachers enrolled and trained.

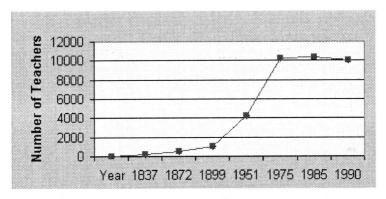

Figure 16: Elementary School Teachers in Jamaica 1837-1990
(Source: *Miller 1986:51*)

Teacher training was a means of social mobility with Blacks being able to avoid agricultural and trading vocations and join the middle class positions of teachers, principals, pastors, and civil servants or further their education at university colleges. The establishment of schools for children of former slaves coupled with the opportunities for the most successful students to become teachers represented a qualitative difference from what existed during slavery. By 1891, elementary school teachers formed the largest single occupational group of those categorised as professional workers in colony because education was the largest social service in the colony at that time.

The Church initiated teacher training in Jamaica and at all times during the period 1865-1999 was the leading producer of teachers.

Theological and University Education

The Baptist denomination decided not to be an imitation of the colonial church, but to be a church that understood her context and roots and became localized in 1842 by declaring independence from the British Missionary Society (BMS). This bold declaration of independence of the Jamaican mission under the leadership of Englishmen, William Knibb and Thomas Burchell, meant that funding of the work had to come from the shallow pockets of the Blacks, and so released about a third of the BMS allocation to other causes while releasing the Jamaican leadership, albeit white and foreign, from the obligation of referring all decisions to London. It also provided the platform for the Church to make new choices, including the evangelisation of Africa and the establishment of theological education. Therefore, in 1843, the Calabar Theological College was established to train Blacks as pastors and missionaries. This initiative was a sign that there was a new self-awareness and self-belief among the freed people, and a recognition from early that the Blacks could manage and benefit from theological education.

The United Theological College of the West Indies (UTCWI) came into inception in 1966 when the Calabar Theological College (1843) united with St Peter's College (1916) and Union Theological Seminary (1954). UTCWI made it possible for locals to study for a theological degree in the Caribbean instead of externally. This degree qualified the graduates to play leading roles in college administration and faculty replacing expatriates. The lectures at UTCWI, and most other theological institutions, were more relevant to Christian ministry in the Caribbean because the material was indigenous. UTCWI produced graduates with a deeper understanding of the nature of the West Indian society and who conceptualised a Caribbean theology and documented local history from the perspective of a West Indian.

There were other theological institutions namely:

- Jamaica Theological Seminary
- Caribbean Graduate School of Theology
- Salvation Army Territorial Training College
- Jamaica Bible Institute of the Church of God
- West Indies College
- Jamaica Bible School
- St Michael's Seminary
- Jamaica Apostolic Bible Institute
- Caribbean Bible Institute (with three campuses)
- International University of Biblical Studies

These theological centres have produced thousands of pastors, who, because of their training, have helped to facilitate community development through quality indigenous leadership. By 1865 there was a cadre of 400 native church leaders who were literate pastors - thanks to education. Schools were the nurseries for the development of leaders in the missionary congregations. They were the start of a new class of Blacks and Coloureds who would take charge of their destiny and form the base for a middle class.

At the dawn of the twentieth century, the Moravian denomination also became localized when at the General Synod of the Moravian Church held in Germany in 1899, the Jamaica Province and East West Indies Province became a Home Province with its own Provincial Elders' Conference (PEC) or governing body, while the General Synod retained a veto power. By 1909 the Moravians became self-propagating, with the right to have its own forms of worship; self-supporting, having control over its own funds and self-governing, being able to enact its own laws.

By 1942 more than one half of the denominations in Jamaica were self-supported largely on a subsistence economy. The process of the localization of the Anglican denomination climaxed in 1957 when the name of the denomination was changed from the Church of England in Jamaica to the Anglican Church in Jamaica in the Province of the West Indies. The Methodists became autonomous in the Caribbean in 1967, and 30 years later the Jamaica District became independent. Theological education had produced leaders who were not inferior to those produced in distant lands and who felt that it was time for local leadership to be responsible for the administration of the Jamaican Church.

To further the process of Jamaicanisation was the development of sections of the Bible in the tongue of patois, the Jamaican dialect. Since 1955, Louise Bennett's use of the dialect on platform and in print has helped to popularise the dialect and helped it to gain acceptance in the wider society. Thus, it was not surprising that the Bible Society of the West Indies (founded in 1971 to facilitate support in the areas of translation, production, distribution and encouragement of the use of the Scriptures with effectiveness) in 1996 decided to translate sections of the Bible into the local dialect. This development was led by translators who were trained in Jamaica. Having the Bible translated into Patois is a part of the process of the people taking charge of their lives and being able to communicate in their popular tongue without it being viewed as another Tower of Babel.

University Education

In 1843, James Phillippo, Baptist Missionary serving in Spanish Town, the then capital of Jamaica, was the first person to propose the idea of a university for Jamaica. One hundred and five years later, the Jamaica Council of Churches (JCC) played a role in making the decisions, which led to the establishment of the University of the West Indies (UWI). The Church ensured that there was a chapel on the campus. In addition, in 1999, the Seventh Day Adventists converted the West Indies College into the Northern Caribbean University, the third university in Jamaica, and the first one outside of the Corporate Area.

The Church has facilitated access for more persons to benefit from theological education and university education via her role in the establishment of tertiary institutions so that enrolment of the student population has increased by 81 per cent moving from 26,941 in 1995 to 29,276 in 1999.

Elementary/Primary Education

When children under six years old were set free in 1834, the Church established elementary schools for those children and coupled with the opportunities for the most successful students to become teachers, represented a qualitative difference from what existed during slavery. By 1837 the Church had founded 183 elementary schools with an enrolment of 12,580 pupils and 257 teachers (Miller 1994: 50-1). Most of these elementary schools were largely staffed by expatriate Whites and local Coloureds which was facilitated by the Negro Education Grant which allowed teachers from overseas to be paid more than their local counterpart. As early as the 1840s, promising students from elementary schools were recruited as pupil teachers at age 14 and having done apprenticeship as a pupil teacher in the elementary schools would then go on to colleges. At that time there were no intermediary high schools for the Blacks as that was restricted for Whites, Jews and Coloureds. The education system between 1834-1865 saw only elementary education being offered with parents paying for the schooling of their children. This system reflected the pluralism of the society with Church schools being organised as parallel systems delivering the same type of education to different ethnic groups with the Blacks and poorer Coloureds benefiting from Church schools while the Coloureds, Jews and poorer Whites attending endowed schools, which were usually Christian.

With the token assistance of £30,000 per year, which the British government provided the British West Indian territories, the Church built some schoolhouses. When the final diminishing government grant was made to the Church in 1845, it did not prevent the Church from building more schools but rather the source of funding changed to be essentially the offerings from the congregations. After the Morant Bay Rebellion, the State had begun to play an increasing role in education with Governor Sir John Peter Grant using the monies saved from the disestablishment of the Anglican Church for increased provision for education. However, it was the Church that laid the foundation for elementary school system until the government assumed responsibility for the system in 1892. By that time there were already 888 schools, an increase of 340 per cent over what existed 24 years earlier. Errol Miller in *The Marginalisation of the Black Male* states that 'when the government took over the denominational system, the denominations had built 544 schools' (p 68). Based on Table 10, at all times during 1868-1999 the Church has been the major builder of elementary schools, even after the recommendation of the Lumb Commission of 1898 which barred the Church from erecting any more schools for the elementary system.

The government assuming responsibility for the elementary system in 1892 was a result of a shift in thinking and policy in England with education becoming the responsibility of the State and not the Church. Schools were increasingly being financed by local government with recurrent expenses and new schools being built from the coffers of local authorities. This shift in educational policy was copied in Jamaica and there was a concomitant problem in the colony in that the various denominations of the Church were finding it increasingly difficult to meet the recurrent cost of the improved and expanded elementary system. Ecumenical cooperation could have alleviated this burden by a voluntary amalgamation of small uneconomical schools in the same locality that were managed by various denominations. However, the denominational rivalry was such that they preferred to hand over the system to the State than to cooperate with each other. In many villages there were several small schools each belonging to different denominations and the recurrent cost of so many small uneconomic units was high. The number and location of the schools built by the denominations reflected not only demand and need of the children, but also denominational rivalry, which saw education as a major means of increasing church membership. By 1895 there were 962 schools serving 99,790 children, at an average of 104 pupils per school (Miller 1996:70). To approximate the magnitude of the economic error committed by the denominations, one can compare the number of schools in 1895 with the number in 1984. In 1984, there were 800 primary and all age schools catering to 412,000 children in Jamaica at an average of 515 pupils per school, which would be considered an average medium size school. During the 90 year period, the number of schools had declined by 15 per cent, although the school population had increased by more than 412 per cent!

Year	No. of Schools		Year	No. of Schools
1868	286		1879	646
1869	262		1892	888
1870	329		1893	912
1871	408		1894	957
1872	438		1895	962
1873	456		1896	932
1874	500		1897	924
1875	526		1898	913
1876	569		1899	893
1877	583		1900	776
1878	617		1999	796

Table 10: NUMBER OF ELEMENTARY SCHOOLS 1868-1999
(Source: *Miller 1994: 69 and Personal Communication*)

It is against this background that the Church system of education was transferred to the government and became the State system of elementary education by the Education Law of 1892. The effect of this law was that the Church would continue to manage, own and partially maintain their schools while the government would be responsible for establishing a Board of management with responsibility to hire and dismiss teachers; meet all recurrent expenditure for elementary education and impose an education tax to compensate for the abolishment of students' fees. The Church was no longer the sole power in elementary education, having given up effective control of the system, while maintain an active presence and influence with the power to command teachers to perform duties outside of the classroom. By 1892, the Church laid the foundation for quality elementary education, which was delivered to the majority of the children of the black majority. The Church, whenever there was a gap in the public system, made pioneering inroads into the elementary system, for example in February 1916 a bamboo shed was built at Maurice Hill, Constant Spring to serve as a school for the children from the Indian settlements at Constant Spring and Swallowfield. In June of that year, that school was recognized by the government as a Special East Indian School and was supplemented with a grant.

In 1999, the Church was still the major non-governmental agency in the elementary/primary school system, being directly responsible for 256 of the 796 schools or 32 per cent (See Tables 10 and 15).

High School/Secondary Education

The high school education system in Jamaica was established later than in Trinidad or Barbados. This was attributed to the lack of influential Whites in Jamaica who needed that level of schooling. In addition, the ruling white minority strongly opposed high school education for Blacks and Coloureds as part of its overall effort to retain control of the former slave society. The emergence of high school education was due to a shift by policy makers who believed that the middle classes deserved and needed an education superior to that offered to the poorer black classes in the elementary schools and also because the majority of the white ruling minority could no longer afford to send their children home to England to be educated. Errol Miller in *Jamaican Society and High Schooling* convincingly argues that high school education was elitist;

> High school education would be for white, Jewish and brown children, to keep them educationally superior to black children... The rhetoric was that educational opportunity was being provided for those classes that could appreciate it and make use of it (p 63).

Therefore, Law 34 of 1879 used high school education to consolidate the position of Whites, Coloureds and Jews as part of the ruling class in a free colonial society, while condemning the Blacks to the margins on the pretext that that a higher grade of education should only be offered to those classes who would value it. As such in 1879, the Legislative Council passed legislation permitting the establishment of high school education. So Errol Miller in *Jamaican Society and High Schooling* argues that 'the system of secondary education in Jamaica dates from 1879' (p. 56) although there were sporadic efforts by the Church before that date. The Roman Catholics started St George's College for boys in 1850 and Immaculate Conception High School for Girls in 1858 but these Catholic schools were not recognized or widely patronised. The Presbyterians had established the Montego Bay Academy in 1851, which in addition to training teachers, preachers and missionaries, provided a classical education for boys, and up to the 1850s, Wolmer's offered elementary education only. Therefore, 1879 is used as the beginning of high school education because that is the year legislation was passed.

By 1911, when the system was evaluated and reformed, there were 12 schools owned or approved by the government; the Church had Montego Bay Academy, Wesleyan High School in Barbican, York Castle, St George's, Immaculate, Convent High School for girls at Alpha, Westwood High for Girls, and 12 Deaconess Home schools for girls (Miller 1990:97), while there were six private secondary schools operated by entrepreneurs. This meant that in the early period the Church was a major provider of high school education to the 938 enrolled students in 1879, which had increased to 1,544 by 1911. At the turn of the century, the Church schools constituted the core of the private secondary school system and this shift in emphasis by the Church was due to the fact that after the Church passed the baton of control to the government in the elementary education, she increasingly started to focus efforts on developing secondary school education.

The general characteristics of the high school system in the initial period included:

- Autonomy, with the principals determining which students were selected;
- External examinations were the criterion for success of students, teachers and schools;
- Emphasis on academics;
- Preparatory schools were the feeder schools and not the elementary schools;
- Students were from the middle class and schools were largely self-financing.

The Church provided education for the Blacks, in general, and girls, in particular, and also in locations where there were not enough schools, 30 years before the State. Therefore, the strategy of the Church owned schools was to fill the gaps in the public system. Schools like St. Hilda's, Jamaica College, and Wolmer's were reserved for the upper classes and those of the lighter hue. However, there were some Church schools that allowed Black students who had excelled in the public examinations, to enter their high schools. Among these were Calabar High School for boys and Westwood High School for girls. Reverend William Webb founded Westwood in 1883 following an incident in which parents had withdrawn their children from a school that had admitted black girls. He started Westwood for girls of all classes, which was a contrast to the elitist Trust school, Hampton, in the neighbouring parish of St Elizabeth. In addition, in this early period, Church schools were mainly in Kingston, which at that time lacked an adequate number of schools. Meanwhile, by 1911, the government had restructured the educational system so that public elementary education and teachers' colleges were oriented to literacy, numeracy and vocational skills, while preparatory schools led to high schools with an academic orientation and catering to Whites, Coloureds and Jews.

However, further changes were made in the 1920s when a new framework was developed for secondary education, which saw among other things a grant-in-aid scheme for secondary education and scholarships for children living in parishes without secondary schools. Grant-in-aid meant that government would make grants available for secondary schools, once those schools were not operating for profit and these grants were made without interfering with the autonomous system of secondary education. In 1925, Priest Percival Gibson founded Kingston College with the support of Bishop Cecil deCarteret for boys who could not afford high school fees and children of unmarried parents who were not accepted in traditional high schools. Between 1920 and 1943 these grants helped 23 secondary schools and the Church owned 12 namely:

- Calabar
- Westwood
- Cathedral
- St Hilda's
- Happy Grove
- St Hugh's
- St Andrew
- Kingston College
- St George's
- Alpha
- Immaculate
- St Helena's (Montego Bay High) in collaboration with the government.

Ten were owned by Trusts, the remaining belonged to the government. The changes that occurred in secondary education between 1920 and 1943 led to the incorporation of church schools into the public secondary system because of the government's financial assistance of grants. The autonomy of the secondary school system remained unaltered even though government was now subsidizing it. Nevertheless, between 1912 and 1943, the high schools continued to be the institution of the ethnic minorities, the only change being that the range of minorities they served was widened to include all the light skinned minority groups in the society. The dark-skinned minority (East Indians) and the black majority continued to have very limited access to high schooling (Miller 1990:127).

The first significant change for the benefit of the black majority in the high school educational system occurred after Jamaica gained political control through Universal Adult Suffrage in 1944. This meant that political power in the nation was democratised and a similar democratisation of access to high school education followed in 1958 with the establishment of the Common Entrance Examination. 1944 therefore marked the beginning of the transformation of the high school education. As a consequence of economic depression and the subsequent social upheavals of the 1930s, The Kandel Committee of Enquiry and its Report of 1943 recommended that the distinction between classes should be abandoned, requiring that the parallel systems of elementary and secondary education should be abolished. The policy shift articulated was that secondary education was for adolescent stage of human development and not for a certain class of people, and all children should receive a common programme of primary education, which would terminate at age 11 or 12. Post primary education would then be based on the abilities of students and not on the ability of parents to pay the fees. The implication of this new system was that based on ability, black children could enter academic secondary schools and conversely white children could end up in vocational schools and trade training centres. Between 1943 and 1954 four additional secondary schools became grant-aided and student enrolment more than doubled moving from 3,380 to 7,640 (Miller 1990:153). As at 1958, for the first time most students entered high schools based on their performance in the Common Entrance Examination. The prejudicial method of educational streaming was removed with accessibility to all ten-year-old children on a competitive performance basis. Formerly, the government offered parish scholarships and paid for students in these private schools but with the introduction of 'Free Places', it obligated the government to pay, to the private schools, a percentage of the cost of all children who were offered 'Free Places'. Grant-aided schools allowed in primary school graduates based on merit, and so primary school students who did well stood a good chance of advancing to a high school irrespective of which social class they were from. The problem that arose was that there were not enough places for the primary school graduates in the high schools and the UNESCO inspired reforms of 1966 led to the establishment of 50 new junior secondary schools for the age group 12-15 which created another parallel system rather than add space to the high school system. Meanwhile the Church established four schools in that decade one of which was in St Thomas, which got its first high school in 1961 so that children from the working classes could benefit from high schooling. Then in 1973 the government introduced free high school education, pay ing for the total recurrent cost of the schools without recourse to schools fees or voluntary contributions, as the government embraced those responsibilities. Nevertheless, free education did not alter the cornerstone of the grant-in-aid scheme, namely the church-state partnership to provide secondary education but it did heighten the desire for high school education. To address the issue of shortage of space in 1978 the government decided to assimilate the extension schools into normal high schools and the number of students admitted to high schools increased from 6,500 to 9,000 (Miller 1990:163). The Church, on the other hand built two schools in that decade. The classroom shortage remained chronic and by 1995 there were 55,000 primary level pupils seeking 15,000 spaces in secondary schools. To address this problem all primary schools students sitting the Grade Six Achievement Test (GSAT) in 1999 was placed in a secondary school, albeit that some of the schools needed upgrading.

Between 1940 and 1985 there was a rapid growth in the number of Church schools, moving from 12 to 21, which helped to move the number of school in the public system from 23 in 1944 to 46 in 1985, the Church's contribution being 45 per cent of the public high school system. Most importantly, in the 1980s and 1990s Blacks were the majority racial group in the teaching profession, which is reflective of the majority racial grouping in society. By then however, according to Errol Miller race had been replaced by class as a determinant of entrance to high school, 'But class was being introduced as the criterion for access. In 1985, of the children in high schools 84 per cent came from families that should have been able to afford high school education' (Miller 1990:337). This is still better than 1940 when 2 per cent of the high school student population was from the lower classes (Miller 1990:338) and by 1985, this figure increased to 16 per cent. During 1942-1985 the Church owned schools accounted for the majority of students admitted to public schools (See Table 11).

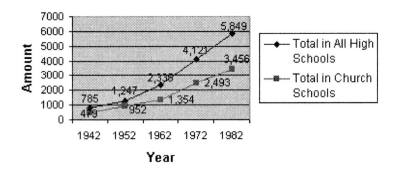

Table 11: Admittance rate in Church owned schools

High school education goes beyond the boundaries of pedagogy and academic achievements to become important sources of identity and social meaning. It is the preferred secondary school to technical high, comprehensive high, agricultural secondary, new secondary and vocational schools, and has a higher ranking than teachers colleges and universities in the eyes of the people. Students define their self-worth and values in terms of the high school attended and it facilitates access to other social groups and linkages to economic opportunity (Miller 1990:339).

The Church, as providers of high school education, has been the major agent of change since the establishment of high school education in 1879. The Church has facilitated a better distribution of high schools throughout Jamaica (See Figure 17).

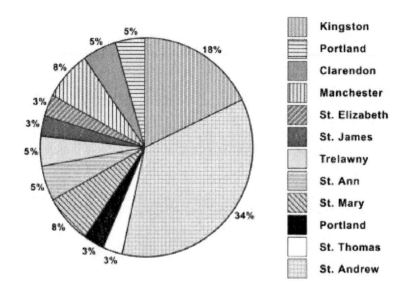

**Figure 17: Distribution of Public Church Schools
According to Parishes**
(Source: *The Ministry of Education and Culture 2000*)

It is true to say that it is the Church that led the way in the provision of space and the opportunity by establishing several high schools, especially after 1897 (See Table 12).

Parish	Schools	Denomination	Founded
Kingston	St George's College	Roman Catholic	1850
St Andrew	Immaculate Conception High	Roman Catholic	1858
St Ann	York Castle	Methodist	1875
Trelawny	Westwood	Baptist	1882
Kingston	Convent of Mercy	Roman Catholic	1888
Portland	Happy Grove High	Quakers	1898
St Andrew	St. Hugh's	Anglican	1899
St Ann	St Hilda's	Anglican	1906
St Andrew	Calabar	Baptist	1912
Manchester	DeCarteret	Anglican	1920
St Andrew	Merle Grove	Gospel Assemblies	1924
Kingston	Kingston College	Anglican	1925
St Andrew	St Andrew High	United/Methodist	1925
St James	Mt. Alvernia	Roman Catholic	1925
St Mary	Marymount High	Roman Catholic	1935
St Andrew	Holy Childhood	Roman Catholic	1937
Clarendon	Clarendon College	United	1942
St Andrew	Oberlin High	United	1946
Manchester	Knox College	United	1947
St Andrew	Ardenne High	Church of God	1948
St Catherine	St Catherine	Roman Catholic	1948
St Mary	Iona	United	1949
Kingston	Excelsior	Methodist	1951
Kingston	Holy Trinity	Roman Catholic	1953
St Andrew	Queen's	Anglican	1954
St Mary	St Mary's College	Roman Catholic	1955
Kingston	Camperdown	United	1958
St Andrew	Meadowbrook	United	1958
Clarendon	Glenmuir	Anglican	1958
St Andrew	Dunrobin High	Gospel Assemblies	1959
St Catherine	St Jago	Anglican	1959
St Andrew	Campion College	Roman Catholic	1960
St Thomas	Morant Bay High	Methodist	1961
Trelawny	William Knibb	Baptist	1961
Manchester	Bishop Gibson's	Anglican	1962
Kingston	St Anne's	Roman Catholic	1973
St Andrew	Edith Dalton James	Gospel Assemblies	1977
St Elizabeth	Black River High	Anglican	1986

Table 12: Church High Schools

(Source: *The Ministry of Education and Culture 2000 and Personal Communication*)

Independent High Schools

The establishment of ten independent high schools in nine parishes (See Table 13) was part of the Church's commitment to education. These independent high schools are not public education institutions, so the government cannot determine who attends, however, these give students access to secondary education who could not find space in the traditional high schools, though at a cost. These independent schools are owned and managed by the Seventh Day Adventists who have deliberately stayed out of the public system and operate its institutions through fees and voluntary contributions from the Church, a means that is neither novel or unique to this denomination but rather the way the earlier denominations had operated until they were incorporated into the public system.

High School	Parish	Founded
Riverside	St Catherine	1907
West Indies College High	Manchester	1919
Kingsway	St. Andrew	1944
Harrison Memorial	St James	1953
May Pen	Clarendon	1954
Willowdene	St Catherine	1962
Portland	Portland	1962
Savanna-la-Mar	Westmoreland	1967
Port Maria	St Mary	1969
St Ann's Bay	St Ann	1972

Table13: Independent High Schools
(Source: *The Ministry of Education and Culture 2000
& Personal Communication*)

Early Childhood Education

Early childhood education encompasses organised activities for children from the age of four to six, an age group which educators claim is the most creative years of a person's life. To cater to the needs of that stage of development there were basic schools, infant schools, infant departments and preparatory schools. An infant school is a pre primary institution for which government has full responsibility for recurrent and capital expenditure including paying the teachers and maintaining the campus. In addition, infant schools have their own principal. In 1983, there were 29 such schools in all parishes except St Andrew, St Thomas and St Elizabeth with an enrolment of 10,566 pupils. On the other hand, an infant department is the pre primary section of a primary or all-age school and falls under the supervision of the principal of that school and is usually on the same campus and often on the same building as the primary or all-age school of which it is a part. Like an infant school, the government undertakes all responsibilities for capital and recurrent expenses of this department. In 1983 there were one hundred infant departments with an enrolment of 7,670 pupils. Preparatory schools are neither government nor community schools but are rather independent bodies falling under the supervision of the Registrar of Independent Schools. These preparatory schools, including the 26 Church established ones, charge exorbitant fees. The Roman Catholics are responsible for 19 of them (See Appendix VI).

It is however, the basic schools that cater to most children in that age group, and it all began when co-founder of the Meadowbrook High School, Reverend Henry Ward, founded the first basic school in Islington, St Mary in 1938 because he wanted to save the scores of children left unprotected while their parents were at work. This action was timely because of the prevailing economic conditions and most of the children who attended basic schools were socially and economically disadvantaged. So through the instrumentality of Henry Ward, a committee was set up by the government that studied infant education in Jamaica and made recommendations, which led to the establishment of an infant centre in Kingston. Public opinion was so stirred concerning needy children, that many villages and towns followed the Islington example by establishing infant centres, which later became known as basic schools. The Church and other charitable or voluntary organisations sponsored many of these centres.

Basic schools are community schools in which the community establishes and sponsors them. The teachers in these institutions are generally not qualified and their role is to be mother substitutes giving excellent emotional support while teaching motor skills and verses of scriptures and songs. Basic schools fall into two categories namely recognised and unrecognised. The recognised being schools that receive financial assistance from the government for teachers salary subsidy, nutrition subsidy, appliance, furniture and building grants, while the unrecognised ones receive no financial assistance. In both cases, the schools charge fees to help pay the teachers and were supervised by the Early Childhood Unit. In 1983, there were 1,108 recognised basic schools with an enrolment of 82,028 and 354 unrecognised basic schools with an enrolment of 15,978. The basic school programme has been enhanced by the Bernard Van Leer Foundation of the Netherlands which in 1966 initiated the first early childhood project with the helpful guidance of Deacon Dudley R B Grant that helped to train teachers, develop a suitable curriculum and designed proper aids to make the curriculum effective. This was further enhanced by the Ministry of Education's Five Year Plan (1978-1983) which had objectives to:

- Identify social, intellectual, physical and emotional needs of the child and develop and implement programmes to meet those needs
- Provide at least a minimum nutritional level for children
- Cooperate in developing and maintaining continuous research and evaluation of teaching and learning activities in early childhood education
- Assist the community in its mobilization of resources
- Help parents understand the specific role they can play in the total growth of their children.

Another boost for basic schools was the European Economic Development Fund, which provided accommodation for 3,000 pupils by building 28 new basic schools and upgrading 75 older structures between 1978-1983. The North Coast Project (1987-1994) has helped to upgrade the skills of the teachers who are now far more qualified than in previous years. According to *The History of the Basic School Movement in Jamaica*, by 1999 at least eight out of every ten Jamaican children attend basic schools, and by the end of 1997 some 3,500 teachers had been trained to look after some 130,000 children in 1,700 Basic Schools. This is phenomenal growth from the humble beginnings of 1938 and with the Church developing an enviable record in building basic schools. In addition, according to the Ministry of Education's 2000 report the Church was responsible for 336 basic schools.

Table 14 shows steady growth between 1995 and 1999 of which the Church was a significant contributor. The 1999 figures are truly impressive when it is compared to what existed in 1865. If a Jamaican can read and write, has a high school certificate, teacher's certificate, diploma or university degree he or she should say thanks to the Church for her contribution in the development of Jamaica's education system.

	1995	1996	1997	1998	1999
Early Childhood *	16,440	15,155	16,238	16,953	17,049
Primary	300,931	293,863	302,090	302,057	309,808
Secondary	221,831	214,313	227,222	228,950	226,384
Tertiary	26,941	26,988	26,193	25,181	29,276
Total	566,143	550,319	571,743	573,141	582,517

*These figures do not include pupils who attended basic schools and preparatory schools

Table 14: Student Enrollment by School Level 1995-1999
(Source: *The Gleaner, January 31,2002*)

Literacy

Literacy is the acquisition of reading and writing skills and the earliest efforts at addressing the issue of literacy in Jamaica were geared to teaching adults through Sunday Schools on the plantations during slavery. During slavery, teaching slaves to read was seen as a subversive activity by the planters and slaves who learnt to read and write did so covertly and the missionaries who taught them did so at their own peril. Then in 1834 following the abolition of slavery there was the goal of making the adult population literate and mass education in the post-emancipation era included both children and adults, which was consistent with new idea in Britain of schooling its children.

But when is a person literate? Up to 1943 literacy was defined as the ability to recognise the letters of the alphabet, spell simple words and sign one's name but in the Independence era, the definition changed to the functional standard of comprehension of what is read. Jamaica followed the international standard that described literacy as possessing the required levels of comprehension and written expression. Another change was the age at which the skill should be acquired. In the nineteenth century the literacy levels of the population was assessed at five years and over and then in the first half of the twentieth century literacy levels were assessed based on ten years and over and since 1960 the assessment of literacy has been of the population aged fifteen years and over. The changes in definition and age of population make comparisons between different periods difficult at times.

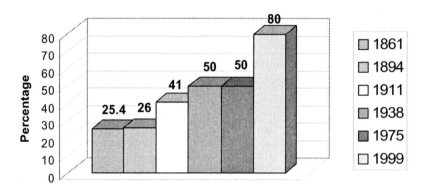

Figure 18: Changes in Literacy Rate
(Sources: *Moore & Wilmot 1998 and JAMAL Foundation*)

There have been many efforts to tackle the problem of illiteracy with the first recorded programme in the twentieth century to address this problem of adult illiteracy being the 'Each one, teach one' campaign launched in 1943. Then in 1951, the Social Welfare Commission (now the Social Development Commission), with the help of UNESCO, started another literacy programme, which led to the development of a local cadre of trained personnel and also produced local teaching materials. After Independence the programme was strengthen and radio and television were used in teaching. In 1972 there was a new government, which established a National Literacy Board with the mandate to eradicate illiteracy in four years, and this Board gave way to the Jamaica Movement for the Advancement of Literacy, popularly called JAMAL. The new government of 1980 brought a different philosophy to JAMAL by integrating it with that of the formal school system. Between 1974 and 1987 JAMAL was instrumental in teaching over 250,000 adults to become functional literate. In fact, there has been a steady improvement in literacy figures from 1861 until 1999 although the figures in the 1861 to 1960 was dealing with basic literacy and after that the measurement was of a higher standard (See Figure 18). Jamaica's literacy rate when compared internationally is just slightly lower than the highest rates that exist globally and is in fact much higher than most countries in the world. In 1980 Jamaica's functional literacy rate was 82 while Canada was 84, the USA 87 and the United Kingdom 88. It was therefore not surprising that JAMAL's contribution to literacy was recognised at the international level by being awarded through UNESCO the prize for being one of the best adult literacy programmes in the world! The Church along with, friendly societies, youth groups, governments and neighbourhood groups have played a significant role in the success of the adult literacy programme of JAMAL.

Buildings for Education

The Church manages 256 primary and all age schools, 43 high schools and 3 teachers' colleges as at 1999 (See Table 15) and 336 recognised basic schools. This table lists the public institutions, as such the Seventh Day Adventists teacher training institution is not listed because it is independent, neither is Mico College because although it is Christian, it does not belong to any one denomination. Coupled with the 336 Recognised Basic schools that are owned by the Church and Trust funds, which built high schools such as Munro, Hampton, Rusea's, Mannings, Jamaica College, Beckford and Smith (as of 1956 it became St. Jago), Wolmer's and Cornwall College, would more often than not had a Christian origin as demonstrated by the usual stipulations for its administration that the headmaster was to be an Anglican clergyman, and the local priest be the chaplain means that the Church owned and managed the majority of school buildings.

Church	Primary/All Age	High	Teachers' College	Total
Anglicans	72	11	1	84
Associated Gospel	20	3		23
Baptists	54	3		57
Catholic	27	11	1	39
Church of God		1		
Methodist	31	4		35
Moravian	43	1	1	45
Society of Friends		1		1
Salvation Army		1		1
United	9	7		16
Total	**256**	**43**	**3**	**302**

Table 15: Church Public Education Institutions, 1999
(Source: *Ministry of Education and Culture 2000 and The Gleaner 2000*)

In addition, Church buildings decorate the landscape of the island with more than 5,000 Church buildings in the island and a sample of nineteen major denominations reveals that they own 2,883 buildings (See Appendix VII) and many of these impressive structures serve educational purposes. There has been no institution that has had so many buildings at the disposal of the populace for educational opportunities. It is in the field of education that the Jamaican Church has made her greatest investment and no other organisation has built more educational institutions between 1865 and 1999 than the Church.

Figure 19: Calabar High School, St. Andrew
(Courtesy of the Gleaner Company)

The educational system by 1999 was of a better standard, more indigenous than in 1865 and far more persons are benefiting from education at all levels: early childhood, elementary/primary, preparatory, secondary and teacher training, theological/university and much thanks has to go to the Church. The Church has left an indelible mark on the slate of Jamaican educational structure in the sphere of traditional high, basic, primary and all-age schools and tertiary thereby equipping the people to assume leadership positions. She has been successful in using education for social mobility as seen in economic empowerment, production of a vast number of teachers, majority of the Blacks are in the high schools and leadership positions in every sphere of Jamaican life. Education as a means of social control has not been as successful, as there have been the Morant Bay Rebellion, Labour Riots of 1938, Rodney Riots of 1968 and gas riots in every decade from the 1970s to the 1990s. However, the

Church has used education as a means of evangelism and in the following chapter the successes of the Church in evangelism will be outlined. The Church was the first institution that provided an opportunity for the education of the freed people through the establishment of Church Schools and this foundation has been built on so that the Church in 1999 was the foremost institution as an education provider.

Figure 20: Boulevard Baptist, St. Andrew
(Courtesy of Boulevard Baptist)

CHAPTER FOUR

EVANGELISM AND VALUES

Go therefore and make disciples of all nations, baptizing them in the name of the Father, Son and Holy Spirit, teaching them to observe all that I have commanded you. (Matthew 28: 18-19)

The main vehicle that the Church used in inculcating values was evangelism. Evangelism is based on the belief that a relationship with Jesus Christ allows a person to reject an old and destructive value system based on drug abuse, irresponsible sexual behaviour, poor family life, corruption, and take on a new value system based on respect for life, people and property, family life and healthy sexual practices. The Church has seen evil, heard evil, done some evil things, spoken against evil and offered forgiveness from evil through a relationship with Jesus. The Church is concerned with both individual behaviour and institutional injustices.

Crusades for Good Living

Between 1868 and 1908, the missionary denominations entered a period of growth and spiritual strength through renewed, vigorous and widespread evangelistic effort. The next big islandwide effort was in 1950, when the Jamaica Council of Churches launched an evangelistic campaign with night-time open-air meetings, lunchtime meetings in the streets, business places and factories under the slogan, 'Christ for Jamaica'. There was another, the National Evangelistic Crusade in 1978, which under the slogan, 'Crusade for Righteousness' conducted evangelistic services throughout the island. The call was for the nation to exalt righteousness and turn away from sin.

In addition, there has been a plethora of big gospel crusades, which have included such international personalities as former gang member Tom Skinner, Leighton Ford, Ralph Bell, Franklyn and Billy Graham of the Billy Graham Evangelistic Association. Billy Graham came to Jamaica in 1958 while his son, came 42 years later. It is estimated that, of the 220,980 persons who attended the islandwide Franklyn Graham crusade, 26,124 made the decision to follow the example of Jesus Christ. Other significant international crusaders who visited included German-born Rennard Bonnke (1993); Benny Hinn (1999); the world's most popular and well-known charismatic preacher, Jimmy Swaggart (1985); Argentinean-born American, Luis Palau (1994); and the faith healers, Oral Roberts (1960s) and son Richard (1983).

In addition, Jamaica has seen its share of odd crusades and crusaders. In 1962, for instance, there was the unusual occurrence of six young women becoming variously blind, dumb and crippled after they 'received the Spirit' at a crusade worship service held at the Bible Church of God, May Pen. Under the ministry of evangelist Lucia Howe, however, they recovered (*The Star*, February 14, 1962). Alexander Bedward, was an odd character, famous for proclaiming that he would fly to heaven in December 1920. He had a following of 6,000 who came to him to be dipped in the Hope River and be healed, body and soul. Similarly, Bishop Mary Coore, known nation-wide, led crusades where many claimed to be healed from merely having her shadow pass over them.

Most of the 5,000 congregations host an annual evangelical crusade with thousands being converted. The primary aim of these crusades is to point people to a better way of life and they have succeeded in bringing many persons into the fellowship of the Church, who would otherwise not be found in a house of prayer.

Family Life and Sexual Activity

The family is the smallest, yet most fundamental unit of the community. In recognition of this, the Church has consistently campaigned and provided retreats aimed at strengthening and rebuilding families. The Church has helped families learn to communicate effectively, express feelings constructively, settle conflicts justly, and has encouraged partners to find ways to affirm each other and solidify existing relationships.

The problem of unhealthy family life has roots in slavery, when Blacks were not allowed to marry and were not encouraged to value family life. However, by 1840, when the Free Villages brought about a change in family structure, marriage rates rose within the black population with 10,000 couples formalising their union. Nevertheless, as late as 1942, 72 per cent of children were born outside of legal unions. Mrs Mary Morris Knibb, the first woman to be elected to the Kingston and St Andrew Corporation, and Lady Molly Huggins formed the Jamaica Federation of Women (JFW) in 1944 with one of the goals being the execution of mass weddings. They encouraged women who were living in common law unions to get married for the purposes of empowering themselves and securing property rights for themselves and their children. In spite of this, the problem persists: the most common family unit is the common law union and the majority of children do not have their fathers' names on their birth certificates. Although more than half of the population sprang from common law unions, it is unfortunate that the Church has tended to neglect these types of families.

Another shortcoming of the Church is that it has been viewed as inflexible when dealing with difficult social issues, especially concerning divorce, artificial contraception, sexuality and homosexuality. For example, in 1952, a Church Synod forbade the remarriage of divorced people and unbaptised persons, and some members of the Church community still frown on artificial means of birth control.

Sex education has been a strong emphasis of the Church but with weak results, considering the number of children born out of wedlock and the rapid spread of STDs, particularly AIDS. The Church has encouraged chastity before marriage and fidelity after marriage as being the best strategies for a wholesome family life and in the fight against STDs, but the Ministry of Health launched a campaign in 1993, which emphasised condom use as the best way to fight the spread of AIDS. The Church warned that a campaign to 'condomize' teenagers would fail because the false impression was given that condom usage gave a 100 per cent protection against contracting AIDS. Furthermore, Church leaders predicted that a condom campaign targeting teenagers would be a waste of taxpayers' money based on US statistics, which showed that similar 'Safe Sex' campaigns failed to encourage most teenagers to use condoms properly, if at all. By 1999, condom sales in Jamaica had increased dramatically from eight million to ten million, yet the AIDS infection has shown an equal growth rate (See Figure 21) and the number of people who have lost their lives to this disease has risen (See Figure 22). Nor does the disease show any sign of abating, as 30,000 people are currently infected with HIV and 15 out of every 1,000 pregnant women test positive.

In 1998 the National Family Planning Board (NFPB) recommended that the medical profession be allowed to issue contraceptives to children under the age of 16 without parental consent as a response to the alarming trend of sexual activity among the young. (The average age for first sexual contact for girls is 16 and for boys it is 14). The document, 'A Strategy Outline for an advertising Programme for the prevention of AIDS and other STDs', stated that its first objective was, "to increase the use of condoms in 'new primary' relationship, especially in the age group of 15-39". Interestingly, this proposal runs contrary to the law of the land that states that it is illegal for anyone to have sexual intercourse with a person 16 years or younger.

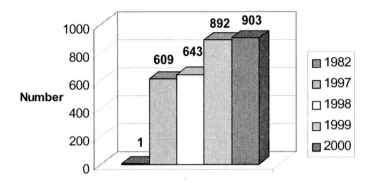

Figure 21: AIDS Cases in Jamaica
(Source: *The Ministry of Health 2000*)

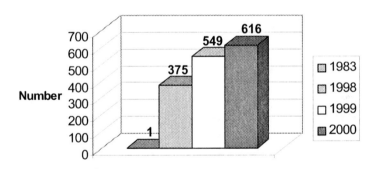

Figure 22: AIDS Deaths in Jamaica
(Source: *The Ministry of Health 2000*)

The Church's position on the issue of homosexuality has been to support those with homosexual tendencies without condoning lifestyle. Church leaders believe that the complementarity of the man/woman relationship is the correct and mode of sexual behaviour. However, tolerance for consenting adults, rather than imprisonment, has been advocated as a concession to a behaviour lifestyle that is an affront to societal norms.

Drug Abuse

The West Indian Commission in *Time For Action* states, 'Nothing poses greater threats to civil society in CARICOM countries than the drug problem and nothing exemplifies the powerlessness of regional governments more' (p. 143). Drug abuse is detrimental to society and harmful to the individual in a number of ways - physically, mentally and emotionally. Cocaine usage in Jamaica has increased since the first conviction of a Jamaican for cocaine possession and trafficking in 1975. By the laws of the land it is illegal to smoke, sell, cultivate or export the popular marijuana, also known as ganja or 'weed'. However, its general social acceptance poses an interesting dilemma for the Church and lawmakers, especially since the derivatives of the plant have been shown to have medicinal value (as shown by the research of two Jamaican scientists, Professor Manley West and Dr. Albert Lockhart). Some Christians swear by the beneficial health properties of ganja 'tea'. In some communities, ganja dealers have become 'godfather' figures because of the aid they give to those in need by helping to pay for school fees, lunches, clothing and school supplies.

The Church has tended to view ganja as a relatively harmless drug, nevertheless it is aware of the negative effects it has had on those who use it - some students have become dropouts or under-achievers, while others have developed mental disorders after engaging in ganja smoking.

The Church has actively participated in the war against drug through community action, rehabilitation, the support of law enforcement, the fostering of drug awareness and by teaching healthy strategies for coping with the stresses of life. The Inter Schools Christian Fellowship was set up in schools with the aim of providing young people with spiritual guidance. One of its focuses was to encourage the students to avoid drugs and this programme has proven very successful.

Communicating Values Via the Media and Music

The Church has used radio, newspaper and television to communicate values to the nation. Beginning in the 1950s, there were Sunday worship services on ZQI and Radio Jamaica as well as religious programmes, such as The Hour of Decision, Back to the Bible and the Lutheran Hour. Now, family counsellors offer help to people in need over the airwaves and religious writers offer critical analyses and commentary on Church and society. Increasingly, other media, such as television and cable have been used as a means of spreading the gospel.

The Church's involvement with the media deepened on Valentine's Day in 1993, with the arrival of Love FM - Jamaica's first religious radio station. The station is owned by the National Religious Media Commission whose membership consists of the Jamaica Council of Churches, the Jamaica Association of Evangelicals, The Jamaica Association of Full Gospel Churches, the Jamaica Pentecostal Union Apostolic, The West Indies Union of Seventh Day Adventists and the Church of God in Jamaica. In this Commission, each member has equal opportunity to contribute to the structure, development and management of the station. A few months after start-up, the All Media Survey, conducted by Market Research Services, the leading pollster on listenership, viewership and readership, claimed that Love 101 had 7.3 per cent of the island's listenership. Since then, listenership has grown to 13.8 per cent (See Figure 23). That same survey found that Love 101 consistently attracted an audience of 14 per cent, which is a good performance for the youngest national station in the field.

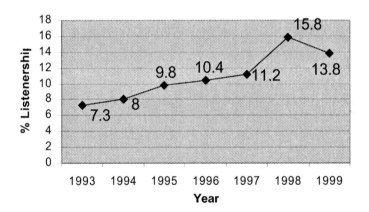

Figure 23: The Performance of Love 101
(Source: *Ridgard 2000*)

At its inception, Love FM 's programming was 90 per cent local. However, only 30 per cent of the musical fare was indigenous. The arrival of the gospel station helped to popularise gospel music and create a demand for it so that, by 1999, the station was playing 50 per cent local music. Love 101 has enhanced the life of the nation with its emphasis on wholesome values and harmonious relationships. It has, since its inception, given birth to a religious television station, Love TV.

Since the latter part of the 1990s, the Church has operated two community radio stations: Roots FM 96.1 and The Breath of Change FM 88.5. The former is aimed at giving a voice to the people of the inner cities and ministering effectively to these citizens in a way that is accessible to them, while the latter caters to those with more traditional tastes. Since 1991, the Church has aired 30-second positive messages on television stations to promote and encourage wholesome family values. The print media has also served as a useful tool in the Church's campaign to reach the masses.

The most popular instrument in bringing the gospel to the young, however, has been through music. Music can make people unwind, release inner tension and stress and can create a pleasant atmosphere for meditation, reflection and renewal thereby healing the mind and invigorating the body. It has inspired persons to great action and encouraged persons to convert to Christianity. Congregations use music that is infectious and persuasive to enrich their services. The Grace Thrillers, a band of musicians and singers, formed in 1975, brought a different style to gospel presentation with the use of keyboards, guitars and drums. Other groups that have had a significant impact include the Love Singers, David Keane and the Sonshine Singers and the Jamaica Youth for Christ Chorale. So popular has been gospel music that Genesis, a yearly musical extravaganza, consistently attracts an average of 9,000 people to the National Arena. The crowd response in these instances often rivals dancehall sessions. In 1999, gospel music was the fastest growing genre in the music industry, attracting former dancehall and reggae stars like Judy Mowatt, Carlene Davis, Papa San and Lt. Stitchie. Gospel music's popularity and appeal is also due to the fact that it makes use of modern genres such as reggae, dancehall, hip-hop, rap, rock and country and western. This fusion has had a positive effect in attracting the young.

The Church has used the tool of evangelism as the major means of encouraging proper values. It has transformed Jamaica into a country wherein Christian values are pervasive.

CHAPTER FIVE

POLITICS, VIOLENCE, JUSTICE AND PEACE

Everything for the people: everything by the people; and nothing without the people. (The Honourable Dr Robert Love, 1839-1914)

Back in the 1800s, high on the agenda of the Jamaican Church was the need for persons to be able to exercise their democratic right to vote in an atmosphere free from violence and prejudice. This was a priority issue that was discussed when the gospel was preached and the lessons taught about morality, social mobility and economic empowerment. Having the right to elect one's political representatives and the opportunity to offer oneself for service and leadership were issues related to justice and peace.

The Church wanted the legally freed Blacks, who were seen as 'political nobodies', to have a voice in the Assembly and for the legislature to be responsive to the needs of the underclass. So as early as 1837, missionary William Knibb encouraged the freeholders to become registered so that they could vote. That year, a coloured man, Richard Hill, gained a historic victory and represented Trelawny in the House of Assembly. By 1863, 700 of the 327,000 Blacks had exercised their right to vote. Many, however, were prohibited from doing so because of the exorbitant tax that had to be paid before voting. Paul Bogle and George William Gordon of the Native Baptist Church tried to get around this problem by advancing the tax money to the financially hard-pressed freeholders so that they could have an input in the official elected. In 1863, Gordon ran in the elections and was chosen to serve in the House of Assembly for the parish of St Thomas-in-the-East. Gordon used this opportunity to agitate for the extension of the voting franchise to a wider cross-section of the population and sought to oppose the oppressive socio-economic and political conditions of the island.

Blacks gradually began to increase in power as a larger number of their people gained political power - especially those voted into the Vestry. The Vestry consisted of the Custos of the parish, Justices of the Peace, the Anglican rector of the parish church plus ten vestrymen and two churchwardens who were elected by the freeholders in each parish. It was in the election of the churchwardens to the Vestry that the Blacks could make a difference because that body levied taxes for the maintenance of the jails, the roads, the animal pounds, education and health institutions of each parish.

Figure 24: Paul Bogle, National Hero
(Source: *Courtesy of the National Library of Jamaica*)

Under the old constitution, the governor could veto bills from the Assembly but was constrained by not having any power to initiate financial provisions because the Assembly controlled the finances. In 1866, the Assembly was abolished and Jamaica became a Crown Colony whose political and financial control was in the hands of the governor. To assist him was an all white panel of six appointed government officials and three others, elected from the plantocracy. Until 1890, there were no Blacks in the Legislative Council, though a few had won seats on the Parochial Board. Nevertheless, the Crown Colony government was more protective of the unrepresented Blacks and made an effort to address their concerns about land tenure, education, health and the administration of justice.

During Crown Colony rule, professional associations like the Jamaica Union of Teachers (1894) and the Jamaica Agricultural Society (1895) were founded, and these organisations were pivotal to Blacks attaining political independence. They were comprised of educated professionals, mainly church leaders, who identified with the peasantry and provided community leadership and political representation. The Jamaica Union of Teachers, for example, opposed the re-imposition of fees for children six years and younger at the turn of the century.

Throughout this period, the Church continued its drive for black political and social empowerment. One of the most colourful and popular religious leaders was Alexander Bedward, leader of the Jamaica Native Baptist Free Movement, who, in 1921, opposed British rule and tried to effect a change in governance by leading a march of 6,000 people from August Town to Kingston. They were specifically protesting against poor living conditions of Blacks and the colonial government's anti-black policies. The government and the established church, saw this protest as a threat and thought it akin to the Morant Bay Rebellion. Bishop Enos Nuttall responded by leading a march against Bedward, who was later arrested, tried and sent to Bellevue Hospital, a place for the mentally ill. Bedward subsequently, died of chronic bronchitis in 1930 and his death led to the demise of this particular church-based political movement.

In the 1930s, the Methodists, led by Armon Jones, Chairman of the (Methodist) District, aided the formation of one of the prominent political parties in Jamaica, the PNP, which was launched in 1938 with the purpose of lobbying for land settlement, universal adult suffrage and social legislation. The PNP successfully made this a reality in 1944 when Jamaica was granted a new constitution that gave Jamaicans Universal Adult Suffrage. This meant that each adult was given the right to vote irrespective of gender, race or financial status. Interestingly, Jamaica accomplished this feat before the United States. This new constitution allowed for an elected black majority in the legislature who was answerable to the nominated Executive Council, while Jamaica was answerable to the British Colonial Office, which meant that final decision-making power was outside of the shores of this island. Church leaders contributed to the political process in different ways. Bishop Percival Gibson served on the Legislative Council with distinction in the 1950s and, during his tenure, the Anglican Church became the voice of the poor and the powerless and was not just the voice of the ruling class.

By 1953, there was a revised constitution, which deemed ministers of government responsible for carrying out the decisions of the elected legislature and further progress came in 1957, when an elected Cabinet, which was presided over by the Chief Minister, replaced the nominated Executive Council. This meant that the citizens had a say in who became members of the Cabinet. Yet Jamaicans were still seen as 'hewers of wood and drawers of water', carrying the responsibility for the activities of the island but without the authority to direct and control it. The following year, Jamaica gained greater authority when the Cabinet was made accountable for all internal affairs. However, matters relating to defence and international affairs were still in the Queen of England's domain. At midnight August 5, 1962, in a moving ceremony at the newly built National Stadium, there was the lowering of the Union Jack and the hoisting of the black, green and gold flag of Jamaica. With that symbolic act, full political power was transferred from England to Jamaica. The right to self-governance was a most significant step on the road to full freedom and nation building, as it was in the 1970s, after Michael Manley had come to power, that the nation witnessed the greatest implementation of social legislation for the upliftment of the people i.e., equal pay, maternity leave with pay - even for unwed mothers - and no discrimination against children born outside of marriage. It is instructive to note that, at this fruitful and dynamic time in Jamaica's history, the Reverend Ashley Smith was serving as spiritual advisor to then Prime Minister Michael Manley. Although the beneficial social reforms cannot be solely attributed to the reverend's influence, one cannot fail to draw the conclusion that he may have played some significant role in bringing about the nation's progress.

By the 1980s, the focus of the Church turned to the promotion of free and fair elections by seeking a moral solution to the corruption inherent in the political system. The snap General Election of 1983 could be said to have precipitated such a response. The story behind that being that the then Prime Minister, Edward Seaga, had called an election without first updating the three year old voters list in spite of his promise to do so. In retaliation, the opposing party - the PNP - boycotted that year's election. In 1984, at the National Prayer Breakfast, Archbishop Samuel Carter, took the JLP and PNP to task and made a declaration 'no more snap elections, no more boycott'. This Prayer Breakfast was instrumental in effecting change, as no more snap General Elections have since been called and no boycotts, even though the voters lists in subsequent years have been less than perfect. In addition, the electoral law was changed in the mid 1980s so that the number of days between the nomination date and the election day was extended to a minimum of 16.

In a further attempt to bring about just elections, Archbishop Carter, on behalf of the Church, chaired the Committee for National Debate which enabled the historic public discussion between P.J. Patterson and Edward Seaga in 1993. Many Ministers Fraternals also facilitated debates at the constituency level to discuss the manifestos of the political parties and programme initiatives. These debates were designed to improve the content of the discussions and reduce the inflammatory nature of the discourse. It was felt that civilized discussions would be a deterrent to violent confrontation, the truth of which seems to have been borne out, as that election was one of the most peaceful in recent memory.

The Church's effort to ensure that general elections were free and fair continued well into the 1990s and beyond. The observer group, Citizens Action for Free and Fair Elections (CAFFE), was born during that time in the rectory of Archbishop Edgerton Clarke. CAFFE got 2,000 volunteers to oversee the 1997 general election. In this way, this organisation ensured that the general elections were conducted in a fair manner. The Church also played a significant role in ensuring fair elections by formulating codes of conduct, monitoring the conduct of candidates, pointing out breaches to the political parties and the country, and helping in the administration of the polls on election day.

The 1990s saw the Church and its representatives attempting a direct entry into the political arena. Such efforts were laudable but short-lived. The formation of a Christian party, the Christian United Party, occurred in 1991, but shortly after its inception it was dissolved. In 1996, Bishop Herro Blair was appointed Chairman of the new political organisation, the National Democratic Movement (NDM). It was a bold move by the charismatic Blair to openly support a political party especially since his Pentecostal congregation eschewed political involvement. His claim that he had received divine endorsement for his acceptance of chairmanship of the NDM, irked many people who interpreted his statement as meaning that God was siding with a political party and guaranteeing NDM's success. Blair resigned after failing to make any significant impact on the NDM or in Jamaica's political arena.

Peace Initiatives Against Violence

1865 was an unusual year in that approximately 500 persons out of a population of 441,264 were killed in the Morant Bay Rebellion and the subsequent government reprisal. This was a feat that made headlines as far as the USA and UK. *The New York Times*, in describing those killings, said that there were 'eight miles of bodies', while in England, the executions incurred such public outrage that the matter was debated for seven years afterwards in the British Parliament. From 1880 - 1915 the number of murders was 20 per year, rising to 25 annually between 1915 and 1958. The homicide rate after the 1960s however, rose to alarming numbers (See Figure 25).

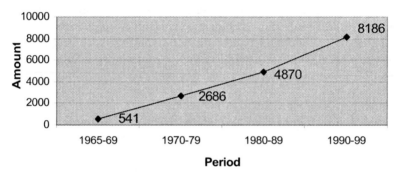

Figure 25: Trend of Murders 1965-99
(Source: *Constabulary Communication Network 2001*)

Since then, several organisations and committees sprang up to address the problem of rampant crime and violence — The Barnett Commission (1976) made recommendations on dealing effectively with crime and violence; The Fraser Commission (1981) and the National Advisory Council on Crime and Justice (1985-86) investigated the causes of and changes in the pattern of crime; and the national task force on crime put forth the invaluable Wolfe Report (1993).

Since the Wolfe Report, 92 of its 102 recommendations concerning the police have been dealt with, 32 of its 35 recommendations concerning correctional services have been implemented and 19 of its 21 recommendations concerning justice have been brought into effect.

In addition to the measures taken by the government to reduce murder rates, the Church has sought, in its own way, to tackle the monster of crime and violence. In the 1970s, the Jamaica Council of Churches (JCC) developed programmes to combat the serious political divisions which had contributed to much of the violence in the Corporate Area. The JCC established a House of Reconciliation between rival political communities, Rema and Arnett Gardens, in 1978. Subsequent to the election mayhem of 1980, which resulted in the deaths of hundreds of persons, many churches and other Christian organisations came together in 1981 and held a National Prayer Breakfast under the leadership of Gerry Gallimore and Reverend Earl Thames. The main aim of this now annual ritual was to play a mediating role between warring communities by targeting their leaders. At the inaugural gathering, Reverend Burchell Taylor, pastor of Bethel Baptist, spoke to the nation about the need for all to request God's guidance in overcoming the country's ills and to ensure prosperity. In addition, Gallimore got Prime Minister Edward Seaga and Opposition Leader Michael Manley to hold hands at the National Prayer Breakfast. That image of unity was expected to herald a new day in electoral peace.

Another peace initiative was undertaken in 1996 when the Roman Catholics launched a crusade against crime, in which Archbishop Edgerton Clarke brought together Christians from uptown and downtown. In 1998, Reverend Stephen Jennings of Mona Baptist called for Christians to join forces in prayer and fasting to bring about the healing of Jamaica. This event, which was held on New Year's Day in the National Arena, was the forerunner to 'Storming the Gates' and 'Jamaica Bawl Out' - two large and public mass movements aimed at stemming violence. 'Storming the Gates', a group of 10,000 people organised by the Portmore Ministers Fraternal marched throughout the communities of Portmore condemning the mayhem and murder in the society and calling the nation to repentance and renewal. 'Jamaica Bawl Out' organised by National Football Chaplain, Reverend Al Miller, was a mass prayer meeting of 14,000 held at the National Stadium, which sought to instigate change away from corruption and other societal ills. These were not the first efforts of the Church to call Jamaicans to turn from acts of violence. On March 22, 1979, the Jamaica Council of Churches had summoned citizens to a Day of Repentance and renewed commitment to Christ and the nation. In 1989, the Jamaica Baptist Union held a National Day of Fasting and Prayer to address societal disintegration.

In addition, the Church supported the efforts of others who sought to bring peace. In 1992, Sir Philip Sherlock, in response to being awarded the Norman Washington Manley Award for Excellence, called for a National Day of Prayer because he felt Jamaica's heritage was threatened by crime and violence. Following that call, the Governor General, Sir Howard Cooke, proclaimed a historic Day of Prayer for Peace and Unity at

Kings House in December of that year. This event was open to the general public and it was the first time that a three-hour prayer meeting was televised live in Jamaica. Now an annual affair, the prayer vigils have brought religious leaders, political leaders and others together in a united effort for peace.

Unity

The various denominations showed the nation their willingness to work together when, on July 30, 1941, ten of them united to form the Jamaican Christian Council - the forerunner to the Jamaica Council of Churches (JCC). The Roman Catholics came on board later in 1971, while the Church of God protested by leaving the JCC because it thought that there were questions about the veracity of some Roman Catholics doctrines. The Ethiopian Orthodox Church, one of the oldest churches in the world, enlarged the family by joining in 1977. This was a rare occurrence to have the Roman Catholic, the Orthodox and the Protestant churches operating as one. This rare union has withstood the test of time, serving to enhance the spiritual, moral, educational, social and economic welfare of the island.

In 1953, five denominations, the Congregational Union of Jamaica, the Disciples of Christ in Jamaica, the Jamaica District of the Methodist Church, the Moravian Church in Jamaica and the Presbyterian Church of Jamaica, started negotiations towards Church unity, and five years later, a paper was presented to the respective bodies for a decision. This body, known as the Church Union Commission, led to the formation of the Union Theological Seminary (UTS), the forerunner to the United Theological College of the West Indies (UTCWI). In 1965, two became one when the Presbyterian Church in Jamaica and the Congregational Union of Jamaica and Grand Cayman merged to form the United Church of Jamaica and Grand Cayman. They were later joined in 1992 by the Disciples of Christ. There was also the Church of the Reconciliation, established in 1969 in St Catherine by the Anglicans and Roman Catholics which allowed them to share the same worship space and engage in joint spiritual, pastoral, social, and fundraising activities.

The Church used that same commitment to unity to encourage the nation toward the formation of a West Indian Federation among the English-speaking Caribbean territories. Bishop Gibson, Hugh Sherlock and other church leaders were supportive of Jamaica being part of this union. It was felt that when the countries united, then they would create a synergy, having greater lobbying strength in the global arena and be better able to develop in the world market. In spite of the best efforts of the Church, the political federation of the West Indies failed. Nevertheless, the Church stressed the importance of co-operation and often displayed unity in many ways. It was therefore not surprising when, in 1969, Jamaica played an instrumental part in the formation of the Caribbean Free Trade Association and joined Caricom (Caribbean Common Market) in 1973.

The church has been engaged in political activism especially before the 1960s, when it encouraged enfranchisement of voters, representatives favourable to the black masses and reviewed legislation. However, the church subsequent to 1960 has largely moved away from representative politics and instead engaged in lobbying against violence and improving the electoral system.

CHAPTER SIX

THE SINS OF THE CHURCH

They did not come to work for their emancipation. In 1865 - and again in 1938 - the Church prided itself on the fact that no Moravians participated in the upheavals, rebellions and riots of the day. (Hastings & MacLeavy)

To portray the Church's contribution to Jamaica's history in a solely positive light would be to give a biased representation. For the Church, much as with other institutions, does have its share of faults and weaknesses. The Moravian denomination's disclaimer that it was involved in neither the rebellion of 1865 nor the riots of 1938 was an attempt to disassociate from justified and heroic rebellion and riots, and this is a general weakness of the Church. Claiming with a sense of pride, no participation in rebellions and riots is a statement that they viewed as evil all these upheavals. No denomination in reflecting on its history has ever claimed that it was involved in or supported the Christmas Rebellion of 1831 or the 1865 Morant Bay Rebellion or thought that the rebellions were justified. Christians will be quick to claim the benefits from the social, economic and political, the end results while disassociating from the means to achieve those ends. This mindset demands that the gospel is preached to win souls while ignoring the slums and squalor in which people live. This is similar to the instructions given to missionary William Knibb, by the Baptist Missionary Society, when he was told not to get involved in the social conditions only preach the gospel, 'have nothing whatever to do with its civil and political affairs, with these you never interfere' (Osborne & Johnson p. 68). Amazingly the Moravians, in reflecting on her history in 1979, at a time of nationalism and social consciousness, could document that they were not about fighting for better social conditions! The Leader of the Opposition, Rt Honourable Edward Seaga also identified the weakness of the Church as a failure to be more involved in political activism on the occasion of the 200th Anniversary of the founding of the historic East Queen Street Baptist Church, when he wrote,

So firmly was the Baptist Church identified with the ordinary people's resistance of oppression, that the Morant Bay Rebellion was called 'The

Baptist War' by some persons. The Church leaders, intimidated by the repression that followed Morant Bay, withdrew somewhat from public affairs but maintained their social activism to encourage faith, thrift and learning. (*Gleaner* Feature May 11, 2000 p. B10)

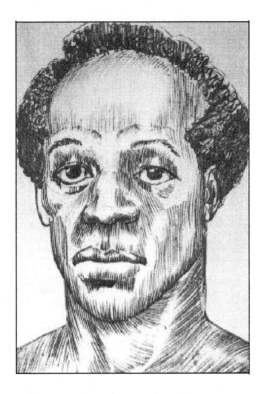

Figure 26: National Hero Samuel Sharpe
(*Courtesy of the National Library of Jamaica*)

However, the usual disclaimer followed those two major rebellions of 1831 and 1865. William Knibb and company said they knew nothing of the plans for the 1831 Rebellion and in fact discouraged their members from such an action even though one of their leading deacons was the chief organizer! After the 1865 brutal repression in which 439 defenceless Black persons were killed, 1000 homes destroyed along with communities, a letter from 58 members of the clergy of the Church to Governor Edward Eyre, chief architect of these crimes against humanity stated:

We the undersigned clergymen of this island, feel strongly called upon at the present crisis to express our deep sympathy with your Excellency, and our utter condemnation of the hasty and uncharitable judgment passed on you...We fully share in the conviction general in this Island, that your promptness, decision, and energy have, under God's blessing, saved Jamaica from possible ruin... *(JRC p. 470)*

These predominantly white clergymen were sympathetic to the British Crown and wanted the status quo of white supremacy over Blacks to be maintained. It was also another attempt by clergymen to wash their hands from taking sides with the oppressed in the Morant Bay Rebellion. However, most Jamaicans rightly associate the Church with these rebellions and the Church cannot wash its hands from knowledge of and participation in these rebellions.

Figure 27: Rebellion at Roehamton Estate, St James
(Courtesy of the National Library of Jamaica)

There is also, an inherent bias by the Church to support the State having faith in the ultimate goodness of those in authority. It was the great philosopher Aristotle (384-322 BC) who said it was the duty of the citizen

70

always to support and obey the State. In the 1950s it would have been common practice at the first business session of Church meetings to pass a resolution expressing loyalty to Her Majesty the Queen with members standing as a mark of respect. The Methodists, in their meeting of 1954, demonstrated this attitude when they declared that self-government is commendable but the Church should not take any active part in advocating self-government. The Methodists were trying to remain neutral by avoiding to take sides against Britain or with the locals for their political independence.

It was also a weakness of the Church to be submissive to the wishes of the State with the ministers of the gospels appearing timid in the face of state power. One such example was in the late nineteenth century when government withdrew funding from Church teachers' colleges that trained males. This led to the closure of Fairfield and Calabar, and the Church closed them without a murmur. Another such example was when preachers were warned to be careful about what they said in their sermons in the aftermath of the Walter Rodney Riots. Following a meeting with the then Prime Minister Hugh Shearer, the Rt Reverend John Swaby of the Anglican communion and Atherton Didier, Chairman of the Methodist District sent out a circular which stated: 'in the present state of security in the country, clergymen should not say anything against the government which would tend to inflame' (*The Daily Gleaner*, December 5, 1968, p. 1). This was being overcautious because there was little indication that the Church was going to say anything harsh against the government as a result of the banning of Dr Walter Rodney from returning to lecture at UWI. In fact, the statement from the Church in reaction to the Rodney Riots was non-committal because she was prepared to avoid saying anything that would cause harm to the government. Anything that seems to upset the status quo is initially like a knee jerk reaction disclaimed by the Church. Also in 1980 at the funeral of Roy McGann, former Member of Parliament, the PNP's song the 'Red Flag' was sung and its value as a Christian Hymn, which came out of the Irish Labour movement defended by the officiating clergy, Reverend Ernle Gordon. Bishop Neville Desouza publicly rebuked him. Was this an instance of a cleric trying to please a political party?

The Church has sometimes inadvertently supported the status quo by the programmes it has initiated and supported. For example, in 1961 Reverend Hugh Sherlock founded and led a Committee for a Better Jamaica with the objectives to develop pride of homeland, dignity, good conduct and hospitality to tourists by Jamaicans. Una Marson rightly describes this as a Courtesy Campaign when what was needed were specific proposals to tackle the bad social conditions of that era. Too often the Church gives a fish when the real need is to be taught how to fish. Too often the Church engages in outreach ministries rather than implementing programmes to challenge principalities and powers and change evil structures. John Wesley, founder of Methodism, began a Christian revolution that altered the moral fabric of the nation by leaving the safety of pulpit and travelling thousands of miles to address the dismal and degrading conditions that existed in Great Britain. Martin Luther King Jr did a similar feat in the United States of America when he advocated for civil rights for the Blacks by making Montgomery, Alabama, Washington Mall and other locations his pulpit. Prescribing a band-aid when what is needed is surgery will cause the patient untold suffering.

Racism

Racism was still a problem in the Church after emancipation. In 1853 Robert Gordon, a black man, applied to Aubrey Spencer, the Bishop of Jamaica, for ordination but the bishop's response was to shift him by offering him a place at Codrington College in Barbados to prepare him to be a missionary to West Africa. By 1865 there was not one black priest. Racism was worse in the Church than in the wider society. By 1860 Blacks had become magistrates, justices, members of the House of Assembly, a coroner, an alderman and vestrymen. Robert Stewart in *Religion and Society in Post-Emancipation* states, 'The Anglican Church was the white man's church not because Whites belonged - that was not the case. It was the Whites' church because the clergy in practice showed that white leadership and membership were its only social legitimisation'. (p. 66). It was a deliberate policy to limit black leadership. The Methodists schism of the 1830s was rooted in racism. There were no coloured pastors among the Methodists. Some missionaries wanted to marry coloured women but they were barred from doing so. In reaction to such racial prejudice Edward Jordan seceded from the Methodist in 1834 to form the Independent Methodist Society. By June 1837, Thomas Pennock, a former Jamaica District Chairman, resigned from the Methodists to form his own Society with about ten coloured leaders. In 1840, the Presbyterians through Reverend William Jameson, trained a number of Catechists for the ministry but all were Scotsmen. In 1859 the Baptists had fourteen local pastors but the E. B. Underhill led British Missionary Society deputation of 1860 recommended the recruitment of more Europeans. This racism bedevilled the Church until the 1950s when black leadership started to assert itself.

72

The growth of black leadership within the Church started in the nineteenth century when in 1845, a white Baptist missionary, Dowson and nine black deacons challenged Reverend James Phillippo for the leadership of the 2,000 strong membership of the Spanish Town Baptist Church over Phillippo's alleged racist comment and writings. However, the ascendancy of black leadership occurred in the twentieth century in the context of the Rastafarian movement of the 1940s emphasising black dignity, beauty and a black Christ, decolonisation in the Caribbean, black power movement in the Caribbean and the civil rights movement in the USA. These occurrences led to a surge of black pride and confidence that locals could do the job. When Jamaica became independent in 1962 there was anxiety among the upper classes of society and prejudice against black people with some even fearing getting a Jamaican passport because some citizens abhorred the idea that a black Jamaican signature would be in the passport. The Church also reflected that prejudice at the time of political independence in that overseas persons were responsible for the pastoral work in the town centres with all the large and prominent churches, such as East Queen Street Baptist, Webster Memorial United, Scots Kirk, Coke Methodist, Kingston Parish and St Andrew Parish having expatriates as pastors. This soon changed; as some of these congregations for example, the St Andrew Parish Church, established in 1664, had its first black and first Jamaican rector in Herman Spence in 1967, and Rhodes Scholar Reverend Earl Thames was the first black pastor of the Ridgemount United Church (1966-69) in Mandeville, and later Scots Kirk (1975-82) on Duke Street, the hub of the capital city. After 136 years of existence the North Street United Church had its first black pastor in 1970, when the young Reverend Raymond Coke took charge. In 1989, the Reverend Randolph Turner became the first black pastor for the Lucea United Church, located in the capital of Hanover. The use of Jamaican trained pastors was facilitated by the departure of many expatriates who packed their bags and returned to their 'motherland' after Jamaica declared independence from England.

R. O. C. King, a pioneer in the ecumenical movement, was the first Jamaican to be president of the Jamaica Christian Council (1955-57). This commenced the process of Jamaican leaders holding responsible positions in ecumenical bodies in the 1950s. Then the Right Reverend Percival William Gibson became the first black Jamaican bishop of the Anglican Communion (1956-67). Also in 1956, Reverend Hugh Sherlock was the first Jamaican to serve as Chairman of the Jamaica District of the Methodist Church, and the first to be President of the Methodist Conference of the Caribbean and the Americas. Samuel Carter answered

73

the call to be the first Jamaican bishop of the diocese of Kingston and in February 1971 he was elevated to serve as the first black Jamaican Archbishop of Kingston. His elevation took place also as a result of the Vatican II ruling, which no longer favoured foreigners holding ecclesiastical offices when competent locals could be found to fill such offices. The trend towards local clergy was important because they knew the language with all its nuances, appreciated the customs of the people and incorporated it in the Church while the foreigners used their European style of worship with its foreign imagery, accent and language.

The assertion of black leadership was under-girded by a cultural renaissance that affirmed black pride and worth. There were the experiments at St Michael's Seminary and Aquinas Centre by Father Richard Holung and Barry Chevannes. Chevannes wrote 'Blak Op' in 1967, which was using folk rhythms to communicate the traditional classical liturgy while Father Richard Holung has grown to present his own compositions in an annual indigenous internationally acclaimed concert in aid of the persons who are poor. Since the 1960s there has been the Mento Masses written by Lisa Narcisse and Matletoft Poule, Reggae Mass written by musician Willie Lindo, Folk Mass and songs written by Dr Olive Lewin, and Folk Mass written by Paulette Bellamy and Noel Dexter. By 1973, Noel Dexter wrote the music for the Patrick Prescod song entitled 'The Right Hand of God' which soon became the cornerstone Jamaican hymn advocating a new day of justice,

> The Right Hand of God is pointing in our land,
> Pointing the way we must go.
> So clouded is the way, so easily we stray,
> But we are guided by the right hand of God.

Dexter has also compiled a *Caribbean School Hymn Book* (1987), which reflected Caribbean National Anthems, songs, and West Indian traditional Christmas hymn, 'De Virgin Mary had a baby boy and dem say dat his name was Jesus'. Easton Lee wrote The Rope and The Cross (1979), which is a Jamaican interpretation of the Passion of Christ in which there is a sympathetic portrayal of the traitor, Judas. In 1973 Father Alfred Reid, rector of the St Jude's Church in the suburbs of Stony Hill boldly commissioned a bronze Negroid crucifix, which portrayed Jesus Christ as a black man. This masterpiece by Christopher Gonzales offended many in the congregation who were accustomed to seeing Jesus through the lens of a Caucasian and by the 1990s this Jesus was rejected and vilified as inappropriate by members of the said congregation. Nevertheless, in other church buildings one can find artwork done by locals such as Barry Watson, Osmond Watson and the late Edna Manley, daughter of a missionary.

This cultural revolution was reinforced by the increased use of drums, tambourine, guitars, keyboards and the only musical instrument that was created in the twentieth century, the Trinidadian Steel Pan, as part of the worship services. In addition, dance groups, chorus singing, clapping and the rhythmical movements of the body are all part of the Worship expressions that is unique to Jamaica and a statement about a new found comfortableness with worshipping Jamaican style as opposed to an European format. Gospel music and bands have also become very important in the popularisation of indigenous music.

There was a cultural renaissance in art and literature from the 1930s and the Church reflected that reality in the 1960s and itself came to view it as a part of the struggle to free herself from colonial forms and racism and to reflect more Jamaican realities and experiences.

Black Racism

There have been race riots in Jamaica aimed at minorities like Chinese by the Blacks. These feelings of prejudice by the Blacks have their genesis in post-emancipation Jamaica when the planters imported indentured workers to force the Blacks to work cheaply on the estates. When the Indians arrived in Jamaica they were treated by the Blacks with similar prejudice and suspicion as the slaves had been treated by their white masters. They were seen as threatening the livelihood of the Blacks because the Blacks saw the Indian as ½ the value of the Black. The planters could get 2 Indians at the cost of one Black. The Indians who were accustomed to a caste system of status based on birth saw the dark skinned workers as their inferiors and some Indians refused to send their children to the same schools as Blacks. In fact, both sides, even up to the 1990s, frowned upon inter-racial marriages.

The Church opposed the arrival of the Indians and unfortunately directed her hatred at the wrong group of persons. It should have been directed at the importers rather than the importees because the Indians too were ill treated. Up to 1938 they lived in conditions which were cramped and unhealthy with only one in every eight barracks supplied with water from either pipes or wells. In addition, non-Christian religions were outlawed and Hindus and Muslims had to congregate in secret. The government also refused to recognize non-Christian marriages and so Indians were obliged to perform Christian ceremonies in addition to their own distinctive customs or their children would be stigmatised as 'bastards' who were unprotected under the Inheritance Law. Thankfully, the law was amended in 1957 to permit non-Christian marriages.

Misguided Rebellion

The Church has also been associated with misguided rebellions. In 1960, the charismatic leader, Reverend Claudius Henry was charged with planning a military takeover of Jamaica. There was also a fear that water reservoirs would have been poisoned. He was convicted and sent to prison for seven years while his son, along with a small band of guerrilla fighters, was captured after an operation in which two British soldiers were killed. The rebels were sentenced to die by the gallows.

Women

Women throughout the ages and the world have been treated as inferior to men. In the USA women were not allowed to vote until 1920; not allowed to pursue a university education until the 19th century; could not hold property until 1875 and were excluded from professions like law, medicine and pastorate. Some of these discriminatory practices were also found Jamaica and there was a time in Jamaica when there was a section in the church building that was reserved for the white rulers and another for the Blacks and the two did not mix. What is not so well known is that there were some church buildings that had separate doors for males and females to enter and exit. This treatment of women as inferior has continued for most of the twentieth century, although the Church now has a positive attitude towards female leadership at various levels. However, on the issue of the ordination of women there are diverse views, with the Roman Catholics and the Brethren rejecting the ordination of women on theological and doctrinal grounds while other groups affirm women in pastoral ministry. The Pentecostal congregations have many female pastors and one such in the group, City Mission, was founded by Bishop Mary Coore in the 1930s. However, except for the Salvation Army, the ordination of women was slow in the mainline churches with historic ones occurring in the second half of the twentieth century, namely the United Church's Reverend Adlyn White (1969), Methodists with Reverend Hyacinth Boothe (1975), Moravians with Reverend Penelope Morgan (1982), the Anglicans with Reverends Judith Daniel, Pat Johnson and Sybil Morris (1994), and the Baptists with Reverend Angela Morgan (1996). Most of these women faced the challenge of not being accepted as being capable of functioning as pastors and there are still congregations and male pastors who will not accept that women are authentic pastors. There are some male pastors who will not invite female pastors to preach in their congregations or participate in the baptism or the Lord's Supper. Nevertheless, women have made outstanding contributions at the pastoral level with Adlyn White, becoming the first female Moderator of the United Church in Jamaica and the Cayman Islands and therefore having pastoral oversight over her male counterpart. Deaconess Elsie Kathleen Bemand, the first West Indian woman in the Wesley Deaconess Order in the Caribbean and the Americas in 1941, pioneered the first Home Craft Centre at Valley Minor that eventually grew to become the St. Ann's Bay Centre. This centre served approximately 400 underprivileged girls. Reverend Madge Saunders co-founded Meadowbrook High School, four basic schools and the Kelly Lawson Trade Centre but little is known about those achievements (Interview with Reverend Madge Saunders November 29, 2001). In 1970 Deaconess Venice Guntley was sent to Zambia while in the early 1990s black conscious Gene Denham went to South Africa in the cause of spreading the gospel.

The story of the contribution of women to the Church and their marginalisation has largely been glossed over. However, the women comprise the largest block of membership within the Church and undertake most of the work. It is therefore gratifying that in the last decade more women have become engaged in the ordained ministry and that there has been greater acceptance of the role they can play within the Church.

The Church has not been perfect and it is also most regrettable that sometimes it has failed to be in solidarity with the genuine cries of the people for justice, equality and prosperity.

In spite of the sins of the Jamaican church, it has done much for nation building in the areas of economic empowerment, educational development, values creation, evangelistic outreach and political activism. Much more needs to be done and can be done, and since so much has been done before with the help of God, the Jamaican church can continue with its mission in the twenty-first century.

CHAPTER SEVEN

THE FUTURE THROUGH THE DOOR OF THE PAST

Be as proud of your race today as our fathers were in the days of yore. We have a beautiful history and we shall create another in the future that will astonish the world. (Marcus Mosiah Garvey, Jamaican National Hero)

The knowledge of the past - its triumphs and defeats - can be a source of inspiration for the future. The past cannot be re-created, but it is possible to learn from the successes and mistakes of bygone days. As Marcus Garvey said, 'a people without knowledge of their past history, origin and culture is like a tree without roots'. A nation cannot gain strength and maturity unless it understands and values its past and applies this knowledge to the present and the future.

In the past, the foundation for nation building was laid through:

* economic empowerment based on land ownership;
* care for the less fortunate and most vulnerable;
* a commitment to educating all children;
* value being placed on all life, respect for God and the community;
* the right to vote in free and fair elections;

The Church, as one of the key nation builders of Jamaican society, must ensure that all these building blocks from the past are maintained and must further articulate new methods for growth and development.

Economic Empowerment

A major problem still facing us today is that of land ownership. In 1999, 400,000 people were identified as squatters and thousands more were found to be anxious to own a piece of the 'rock' called Jamaica. Prime Minister, P.J. Patterson, recognised this issue as a problem and he vowed, at the 57th Annual PNP Conference in 1995, to do something to remedy the situation. His aim was that the PNP would 'go down in history as the government that placed the most land in the hands of the most people'.

It is important for the Church, along with the government, to mobilise the nation and support programmes that will help people without land to acquire land. Land must be made available for the provision of shelter and the development of communities and the Church, with its vast voluntary network, should assist with the re-settlement of squatters and the development of housing. Its job should not end there, however, as equally vital to setting up housing schemes is introducing some sort of community planning. Residents should be shown how to live in communities and should be taught proper maintenance and good conflict resolution strategies. This has been done in National Housing Trust schemes but this ought to be done in all communities. Additionally, land should be used as a springboard for economic stability: Jamaicans should once again be encouraged to take up farming and eat more of what they produce and produce more for others to eat.

When it comes to promoting economic empowerment, business ventures should allow employees to feel a part of the organisation - possibly through the implementation employee shareholders' schemes so that each person has a stake in the business and is allowed a voice in decision-making and policy formulation. This would act as a valuable incentive to direct the people away from 'get rich quick' schemes such as lottery and encourage them to invest in worthwhile ventures. In addition, the Church could play its part by helping those, who would not normally qualify, to secure mortgages or loans from building societies and credit unions by acting as guarantors. This would serve to increase the number of cottage industries and co-operatives and thus bolster the economic development of the nation.

Education

The most immediate need for education right now is an injection of resources. If 2o per cent of the Gross Domestic Product, inclusive of the revenues from the Education Tax, were to be channelled into education, then all children up to the age of 16 could receive an education. The cost of tuition, the cost of sitting CXC subjects and the cost of pursuing further studies would be greatly reduced. It would also allow for better infrastructure with spacious classrooms and better facilities at the early childhood, primary and secondary school levels. This would also go a long way in ensuring parity of spending allocated to corporate and rural institutions as well as at boys' schools and girls' schools at the secondary level. The parents only responsibility would be to provide their children with books, uniform, lunch and transportation. This would indeed be an investment in the future.

The construction of more schools is another area in need of attention. The government, the Church and the private sector together could make this a successful undertaking. The Church should continue to maximise the use of the buildings for educational purposes, including literacy programmes for adults. In addition, the provision of more scholarships and the accessibility of more loans would improve the chances of acquisition of knowledge and skills.

Education should also seek to instil civic pride through the teaching and recitation of the National Anthem and the National Pledge in worship services and school ceremonies. Schools should strive to produce well-rounded students, so vocational and agricultural training ought to be seen as vital components of the educational process.

Values Crusade

The Church is admittedly committed to the practising of wholesome values and continues to crusade for a proper understanding of self, moral consciousness, responsibility to family life, patriotism, community involvement and good inter-personal relationships. The PNP government, in 1996, launched a highly publicised and well-promoted values and attitudes campaign which has, unfortunately, faded in spite of periodic resuscitation. The need for good values, however, has not faded and most citizens expect a level of decency, honesty, integrity and caring to be shown in the society. The Church must be part of that continued process of fostering these shared national values. The country also needs to come to a consensus on some core values such as the worth of all life, what constitutes equal rights and justice and the basic necessities of life, and what is considered a fair day's pay for a fair day's work. In assisting the nation in sorting out the answers to these questions, the Church will propel Jamaica to becoming a more humane, industrious and equitable society.

In building a healthy set of values towards sex, education should encourage the young to abstain from early sexual activity. The message must be sent to sex offenders that coitus with children under the age of consent will lead to imprisonment. Music that glorifies irresponsible sexual behaviour must be rejected along with the excesses of the annual Easter Carnival. Cable television ought to reflect sexuality in a way that is consistent with the ethos and laws of the land and which promote healthy lifestyles.

The crusade for 'right living' must confront evils that affect family growth, development and maturity. These include gambling, excessive drinking and sexual immorality. The needs of minorities who are physically, mentally and emotionally challenged should be treated with respect and these persons should receive the necessary specialised care. Church leaders must continue to tackle other evils such as:

- a political system that encourages corruption and tribalism;
- a slow and cumbersome justice system that is heavily weighted against the poor;
- health services that, by design, practise negligence;
- companies that abuse and exploit workers;
- trade union leaders who unreasonably agitate workers;
- lawyers who exploit their clients;
- bankers who misappropriate the funds of their customers;
- security officers who practise brutality and abuse human rights;
- Pastors who abuse their position and people;
- an economic model that is neither creating enough jobs nor generating adequate economic growth.

Political Involvement

The Church ought to share ideas with the political parties so that they can be incorporated into the political manifestos and parliamentary legislations. The Church must also co-operate with other non-governmental groups that promote wholesome values and continue its advocacy of social justice and equal rights. The Church ought to help to dismantle garrison communities so that there can be free and fair elections, freedom of movement and freedom from crime and violence.

The nation is a plural society and the Church needs to act in tandem with professional associations representative of the society - teachers, farmers, builders, artisans, artistes, sports people, media practitioners, doctors, lawyers and judges, police personnel security guards, auditors etc. - for the promotion of the welfare of the country. The Church can benefit from the specialised skills offered by these associations in the operation of its ministry and mission, while these organisations can benefit in conduct and focus from the Church's ethical insights.

Jamaica needs to reform the upper chamber, the Senate, so that its contribution is less reflective of political appointments and more representative of civil society. This reconstitution would afford the Senate more authority, greater legitimacy and widespread support. The Senate should continue to have the power to delay legislation or suggest amendments to legislations, but the power to enact should be the purview of the House of Representatives. The governing party could continue to appoint 13 persons and the opposition party 8 persons, but the Senate should also consist of the 14 Custodes giving all fourteen parishes a voice. There should also be representatives from certain civic organisations that are mass-based and that have a history of service to nation building and a sensitivity to the interests of minorities. This reformed Senate would be more reflective of society and would benefit from a wider pool of skills, knowledge, experience and expertise.

Community Development

It is said that the death of Reverend M.E.W. Sawyers in 1979 signalled the death of the thriving community of Jones Town and hastened its descent to an inner-city community. For so many communities, the absence of a resident pastor is one of the causes of its demise. Pastors should shepherd the flock and retain contact and remain attuned to the pulse of the community by living among their congregants. Instead, some pastors have fled some communities. So, too, have the politicians. Crime and violence will not abate in these volatile communities until pastors and politicians start again to live with the people for whom they intercede.

The Church's property must be made available to the community as a play area for all ages; as a meeting area for youth groups and other civic organisations; as a place of learning and as a model for the proper use of land for other purposes including tree planting and crop growing. The ministry cannot be confined to christening babies, officiating at weddings and burying the dead, but must continue an activist role of economic empowerment, social engineering and political activity. It is the Church, which stands ready to reconcile people who feel alienated from one another in communities.

The competitive spirit which says 'the devil takes the hindmost' must be rejected and instead it must be affirmed that God cares for all, especially the weak, old and poor. It should not only be the strong who survives, but all who belong to the human race. The thinking needs to be shifted from the survival of the fittest few to the survival of the community. Each member of the community is equally important and has a supporting role to play. The distress of one member is the concern of all.

The Need for Co-operation

In 1999, there were 23 congregations serving 1,000 households in

Guys Hill, St Catherine (Social Development Commission 2000). That means that there was one church for every 43 families. Since one pastor could adequately care for 83 families consisting of six members each, it means that 13 congregations could minister effectively to the community. This means that there are excess congregations in Guys Hill. Yet, in 1995 Guys Hill needed leadership to motivate it to participate in community activities. Guys Hill has the longest history of Community Council in Jamaica, and the Jamaica Welfare Limited of 1938, now the Social Development Commission, originated from that community. What has gone wrong? A better concentration of pastoral leadership could have helped the community to be self-reliant and self-governing. In 1995, the community suffered from 65 per cent unemployment, a dropout rate of 35 per cent from schools, rampant praedial larceny and child abuse and an average of six incidents of domestic violence per month. The community is 'over-churched' yet 'undermanned' - lacking adequate residential pastoral presence. The problem is that when there are too many congregations for the pastor to shepherd, it is more difficult to give personal attention to the parishioners. Such an intermittent ministry results in spiritual stagnation unless the pastor operates like a bishop and has competent lay leaders. But even then, these lay leaders have their own secular jobs to oversee and do not make adequate replacements for a resident full time pastor. When a member of the clergy has to minister to many congregations in various places, he or she is often seen as a mere visitor to a rural community where four or five other ministers are also visitors. This is superficial service and has been an historic problem.

The Church must use its resources better through co-ordination, elimination of waste and reduction of duplication of ministries in any one community. The pooling of resources would lead to more effective ministry and the ability to do more. It must also continue to model unity. Too often the hard work of individual denominations and congregations remain largely fragmented. The work needs to be more united and co-ordinated to better tackle the historic socio-economic problems. There needs to be a greater accord among the major groups of Councils for better and more effective ministry. Uniting the various groups would be a tremendous testimony to the nation as they organise national services, plan national crusades, help in disaster relief, better co-ordinate welfare programmes, concentrate on very poor areas and those prone to violence, create a more structured response to drug abuse, establish new congregations in growing communities and manage the rationalisation of congregations per community and deploy pastors more economically.

From the 1860s, when the population was 441,000, to the 1990s, when the population was 2,314,479 (*Pocket Book of Statistics 1998*), the Church cared for the nation through economic empowerment, education for the masses, political activism and values formation. Of the 5,190 community-based organisations, the Church was the most outstanding of all in economic empowerment, education of the freed and instilling wholesome values. It is the Church with its heightened sense of social responsibility and community that has helped to build the nation by inspiring others through its leaders to create the social and economic associations that encouraged national cohesion and built a nation rooted in morality. There is a difference between living in a place and belonging to it. The Church has helped the people realise that their lives and destiny are directly related to the life and destiny of that of the nation.

According to Carl Stone in his book *Class, State and Democracy in Jamaica*, the Church, as a collective presence, has the largest number of committed members of all the organisations in Jamaica. The Church represents a combined strength of some 32 per cent of the electorate in terms of committed membership. The last census, as reported in the 1998 *Pocketbook of Statistics*, stated that 76 per cent of Jamaicans identify with the cause of the Church. The sympathisers would make the Church, by far, the largest organisation in the island. Mainly because of the Church, Jamaicans believe in God and explain life and phenomena in terms of God. It is a tribute to the role of the Church in nation building that, 'Religion remains at the centre of national life' (Sherlock & Bennett p. 410). This nation, with the help of the Church, will be great in the future because as 1 Corinthians 2:9 states, ' No eye has seen, no ear has heard, no mind conceived what God has prepared for those who love him'.

ENDNOTES

1. Dr Robert Love grew up in the Anglican Church in Nassau and became a deacon. Before arriving in Jamaica he went to Haiti in 1881 as a missionary. In Jamaica, he advocated for greater black empowerment, fair employment practices and equal opportunities for Blacks in the civil service and other public institutions. He started his own weekly newspaper, *The Jamaica Advocate* in 1894 which was the voice of the underprivileged, which publicly challenged the assumption that blackness was synonymous with inferiority. He was a rare Black man to be a doctor. He also advocated for a reformed tax structure and called for self-rule. He campaigned vigorously to get non-white candidates into the Legislative Council. He won a seat in the Kingston City Council in 1898 and 1903 and in the Legislative Council in 1906. This Anglican minister served as mayor of Kingston, chairman of St Andrew's Parochial Board and trustee of Wolmer's school. He was regarded as the most brilliant orator of his day. Love also believed that Friendly societies provided healthy social interaction and a modicum of financial stability for the very poor so he founded the Sparks Lodge.

2. Marcus Garvey (1881-1940) was Jamaica's first National Hero. He pioneered a role for Africa and Africans in world affairs. He advocated race pride and said that Africa was the motherland for Blacks. In 1912 while in England he developed the idea of one great international organisation of educated, financially independent black people who would take their places as equals on the world stage. He formed the Universal Negro Improvement Association (UNIA) in 1914, with its objectives to encourage material success through individual effort; encourage educational attainment, race consciousness and racial pride. Political and religious instruction formed part of the weekly programme. The stated aim of the movement was 'One God! One aim! One destiny!' The UNIA became the largest international organisation of Blacks with a membership of 4 million. He published the *Negro World* (1918), established a political party, People's Political Party and won a seat in Kingston. He formed a steamship company, the Black Star liner with the aim to trade with the Negro race and to link coloured peoples worldwide and enable Blacks to own and operate a steam vessel. He also established the Liberty University in 1926 in Virginia, USA.

APPENDICES

Appendix I: Congregations listed in the Registrar of Companies

CHURCH NAME	Incorporation date
1. Franciscan Missionary Sisters	12-Dec-72
2. Mt Halibeth Christian Churches of the World Incorporated (Halibethian Diocese)	24-Jan-73
3. United Evangelical Council of Christian Churches (Jamaica)	1-Aug-74
4. Baptist Bible Fellowship of Jamaica	13- Jan-75
5. Christ's Ambassadors Church	20- Feb-75
6. The F.B.H. Church of God of the Americas.	22-May-75
7. Berean Fellowship International (Ja.)	23-May-75
8. The Full Gospel House of Prayer Revival Fellow.	23-May-75
9. Jamaica Mennonite Church	25-May-75
10. Gospelight Evangelistic Association	27-May-75
11. Hopefield Christian Fellowship	27-May-75
12. Full Gospels Ministerial Fellowship in Ja	28-May-75
13. United Holy Halibethian Church	28-May-75
14. Holy Mount Zion Revival Church of Christ Kingston	29-May-75
15. Worldwide Church of God	30-May-75
16. Zion New Testament Church of God	30-May-75
17. Church of God In Christ Congregation Indp.	1-Jun-75
18. The Churches of Christ Jamaica	1-Jun-75
19. The First Born Church of The Living God	1-Jun-75
20. The Jamaica Holiness Church	2-Jun-75
21. Sunshine Pentecostal Church of God In Christ	4-Jun-75
22. The Mount Zion Church Of God.	4-Jun-75
23. The Owine Church of God	4-Jun-75
24. The Star Church of God	4-Jun-75
25. Zion Resurrection Church	4-Jun-75
26. Antioch Assembly of Kingston	5-Jun-75
27. Bethlehem Assembly Church of God	5-Jun-75
28. Faith Gospel Association Worldwide	5-Jun-75
29. Holy Trinity House of Prayer of Jamaica	5-Jun-75
30. Life Line Church of God	5-Jun-75

CHURCH NAME	Incorporation date
31. The Bethel Reformed House of God	5-Jun-75
32. The Gospel Fellowship Church of God	5-Jun-75
33. The Little Temple Deliverance Church of God of Jamaica	5-Jun-75
34. The New Covenant National Church of God	5-Jun-75
35. Zion Christian Church	5-Jun-75
36. Bethel United Holy Zion Church	6-Jun-75
37. The Seashore Bible Church of God	6-Jun-75
38. Apostolic United Holiness Church	7-Jun-75
39. Saint Gabriel Apostolic Baptist Church	7-Jun-75
40. The Faith Temple Fellowship	7-Jun-75
41. United Church of Jesus Christ (Apostolic)	7-Jun-75
42. The Central Evangelistic Association	9-Jun-75
43. All Nation Church of God In Christ Apostolic	11-Jun-75
44. Manna Of Life Ltd	12-Jun-75
45. Restored Church of Jesus Christ	12-Jun-75
46. The Miracle Church of God	12-Jun-75
47. Calvary Church of Good	13-Jun-75
48. The Harvesters Full Gospel Ministries	13-Jun-75
49. Cathedral Church of the Living God	14-Jun-75
50. The Christian Connection International	14-Jun-75
51. Bread of Life Ministries	15-Jun-75
52. Holiness United Pentecostal Church	15-Jun-75
53. Inspiration Ministries	15-Jun-75
54. Ministries of the Bread of Life	15-Jun-75
55. B.M.M - The Evangelical Methodist Church of Jamaica	17-Jun-75
56. Church of God of Deliverance	18-Jun-75
57. Dynamic Community Outreach Ministry	19-Jun-75
58. The Angelic Brothers Ministries	19-Jun-75
59. Gethsemane Pentecostal Ministries	20-Jun-75
60. Deliverance Restoration and Miracle Ministries International	21-Jun-75
61. Heartcall Citywave Ministries Jamaica	21-Jun-75
62. Jesus Christ Tabernacle of Prayer Limited	21-Jun-75
63. Pentecostal Assemblies of Jesus	21-Jun-75
64. Power of Faith Pentecostal Ministries Toronto	21-Jun-75
65. The Church of God of Righteousness	21-Jun-75
66. Family Church On The Rock (Montego Bay)	22-Jun-75
67. Global Evangelism Centre	22-Jun-75

68. The Church of God 7th Day Fellowship
    Ministries (General Assemblies)   22-Jun-75
69. City of Faith Church of God   23-Jun-75
70. Gospel On Wheels Ministries International   23-Jun-75
71. Universal Church of the Master Jamaica   23-Jun-75
72. Bridge to God's Glory   24-Jun-75
73. Jubilee Christian Church International, Inc.
    (House of Glory)   24-Jun-75
74. Ebenezer Holiness Church of God   25-Jun-75
75. The Brotherhood of Christ Healing Temple
    of the Full Gospel Tabernacle   25-Jun-75
76. Church of God of the Mountain Assembly of Jamaica 13-Aug-75
77. The Berean Church of God (Jamaica)   6-May-76
78. Zion Faith Healing Church of Jamaica   1-Sep-76
79. Disciples - Oberlin   15-Apr-77
80. Zion Episcopal Baptist Church of Jamaica   18-Apr-77
81. Bethel United Church Of Jesus Christ (Apostolic)   21-Mar-78
82. Olivet Seventh Day Church   20-Feb-79
83. New Life Apostolic Tabernacle Jamaica   2-Mar-79
84. Mount Olive Christ Church Jamaica   13-Mar-79
85. Mount Bethany Gospel Hall   30-Mar-79
86. The Bible Apostolic Church Jamaica   9-Apr-79
87. The Full Gospel Church of God   18-May-79
88. The Living Church of God   22-May-79
89. The Original Glorious Church of God in Christ 4-Jun-79
90. Jamaica Fellowship of Believers   5-Sep-79
91. Triumphant Church of God of Jamaica   5-Dec-79
92. The Jamaica Evangelistic Association   12-Dec-79
93. Redemption Church of God   15-Apr-80
94. Church of God Assembly   6-May-80
95. Holiness Church of God   27-May-80
96. Mystic Holiness Church of Christ   9-Jun-80
97. The Calvary Evangelical Church of Christ   30-Jul-80
98. Mount Zion Spiritual Healing Temple Jamaica 12-Jan-81
99. Holiness Temple Limited   14-Jan-81
100. Methodist Episcopal Church   17-Mar-81
101. The Pentecostal Redeemed Church of God   25-Mar-81
102. Seventh Day Adventist Church Reform Movement 23-Apr-81
103. The Intl. Evangelistic Union Jamaica   15-Jun-81

CHURCH NAME	Incorporation date
104. The Glorious Light Apostolic Temple	7-Jul-81
105. Faith Christian Missionary Church of God	29-Jul-81
106. Faith Miracle Church of God	26-Aug-81
107. The Higher Light Living Church of God	23-Oct-81
108. Holiness Born Again Church of Jesus Christ of Jamaica	26-Oct-81
109. Jamaica Pentecostal Church of God (Trinity)	6-Nov-81
110. Deliverance Full Gospel Church of God	18-Nov-81
111. The Apostolic Church of Good Seventh-Day	30-Dec-81
112. Golden Faith Mount Zion Church of God	5-Feb-82
113. Churches of God in the Fellowship of the Son of God	1-Mar-82
114. Yahvah Little Flock Assembly	7-Mar-82
115. St Michael Revival Tabernacle	24-Aug-82
116. Apostolic Faith Mission	26-Aug-82
117. Church of God Intl. Jamaica	2-Sep-82
118. Fishers of Men Ministries	26-Jan-83
119. The Living Word of Faith Fellowship	11-Feb-83
120. United Church of Jesus Christ (Apostolic)	12-Apr-83
121. Pentecostal Gospel Temple	23-Sep-83
122. Shiloh United Church of Christ Apostolic Worldwide	2-Feb-84
123. Good Life Deliverance Ministries (Jamaica.)	28-Feb-84
124. United Bible Church of God	16-Mar-84
125. The Church of The Lord Jesus Christ Apostolic	23-Mar-84
126. Miracles & Wonder Christ Church of Apostles	10-Apr-84
127. New Testament Assembly	12-Jul-84
128. The Tabernacle Church of God	8-Aug-84
129. 11th Commandment Church John 13-34	4-Oct-84
130. Church On The Rock Jamaica	26-Oct-84
131. Church Services	7-Jan-85
132. Pentecostal Deliverance Centre	14-Jan-85
133. Rastafari Apostolic Church	31-Jan-85
134. The Church of The Living Water	1-Feb-85
135. Faith Christian Fellowship Jamaica W.I.	14-Feb-85
136. The Lord's Chapel	15-Mar-85
137. The Holy Church of The Living God	11-Apr-85
138. The Assemble Holiness Church of God	24-May-85
139. Jamaica Triumphant Church of God	19-Jun-85
140. Faith Holiness Church of Jamaica	5-Jul-85
141. Global Tabernacle Ministries	31-Jul-85

142. St Michael's Apostolic Baptist Church	6-Aug-85
143. The Reorganized Church of Jesus Christ of The W. I	21-Aug-85
144. Bible Centre Assemblies International	28-Aug-85
145. Church of The Living God (JA.)	2-Sep-85
146. Bethany St Peters Zion Sabbath Church	18-Sep-85
147. Mount Olivet Church of Christ The Redeemed	18-Sep-85
148. The Alpha and Omega Church of God	18-Sep-85
149. The Faith Deliverance Church of God	30-Sep-85
150. The Holy Temple Church of God of Jamaica.	8-Oct-85
151. Mt Sinai Fellowship Spiritual Church Limited	14-Oct-85
152. Tabernacle of Prayers For All People	19-Nov-85
153. One Lord One Faith One Baptism	25-Nov-85
154. Church of God Miracle Valley	6-Jan-86
155. Mount Sinai Zion Philadelphia Seventh Day Church	18-Feb-86
156. Miracle Ministry Full Gospel Mission	7-Mar-86
157. Deliverance Tabernacle (Evangelical)	15-Apr-86
158. The Bible Speaks of Jamaica	16-Apr-86
159. Church Of The First Born Miracle Temple	25-Apr-86
160. Salvation and Deliverance Church of Jesus Christ	29-Apr-86
161. Crown of Life Church of God	1-May-86
162. Mystery Church of God	13-May-86
163. Advent Deliverance Church of The Lord Jesus Christ	28-May-86
164. Congregation of Yahvah Company	3-Jul-86
165. The Mount Refuge Church of The First Born	7-Jul-86
166. Holy Tabernacle of Jesus Christ Apostolic Church	8-Jul-86
167. Miracle Church of God In Christ	22-Jul-86
168. The Unification Church (Jamaica)	24-Jul-86
169. Watch Tower Bible And Tract Society of Jamaica	29-Jul-86
170. The Masloth Church of the Living God	8-Sep-86
171. The Power of Faith Ministries	17-Sep-86
172. The Missionary Church Foundation	22-Oct-86
173. Word of Life Christian Fellowship	24-Oct-86
174. Holy Ghost Power	31-Dec-86
175. Advent Sabbath Church	13-Jan-87
176. Christ To The World Ministries	13-Jan-87
177. The Revived Church of God	20-Jan-87
178. United Holiness Church of God	26-Jan-87
179. Bethlem Evangelistic Assembly	10-Feb-87
180. The Community Church of God	13-Feb-87

	CHURCH NAME	Incorporation date
181.	Maranatha Christian Church and Campus Ministries (Caribbean)	6-Mar-87
182.	Calvary Evangelistic Assembly	12-Mar-87
183.	Trinity Evangelical Ministries	12-Mar-87
184.	International Evangelical Mission	25-Mar-87
185.	United Council of Full Gospel Pentecostal Churches	25-Mar-87
186.	The Church of Christ Holiness Unto The Lord	2-Apr-87
187.	Protestant Reformed Churches of Jamaica	14-Apr-87
188.	Kings Chapel Apostolic Church	23-Apr-87
189.	Faith Prayer House Church of God	5-May-87
190.	The Evangelical Church of God	14-May-87
191.	Bethel Tabernacle Church of God	20-May-87
192.	Mount Zion Ministries (Jamaica)	22-May-87
193.	Pentecostal Holiness Church of Jamaica	9-Jun-87
194.	Saint. Joseph Spiritual Church	15-Jul-87
195.	New Creation Ministries	6-Aug-87
196.	Faith & Believe Church of God	17-Sep-87
197.	Shoreline House of Prayer Church of God	1-Oct-87
198.	All Nation Church of God in Christ Apostolic Faith	9-Oct-87
199.	Covenant Community Church	23-Oct-87
200.	The Church of Our Lord Jesus Christ Apostolic	25-Nov-87
201.	The Worldwide Mission Fellowship	17-Dec-87
202.	Jamaica Evangelistic Mission	7-Jan-88
203.	Worldwide Pentecostal Mission Fellowship Jamaica	8-Jan-88
204.	Prayer Line Church of God	14-Jan-88
205.	Mt. Joy Three of Life Apostolic Faith Church	29-Jan-88
206.	The Church of God Pentecostal	22-Feb-88
207.	God's Way Assembly	29-Feb-88
208.	Assemblies of The First Born of Jamaica Church	16-Mar-88
209.	The Church of Christ Southwest Constant Spring	17-Mar-88
210.	The English Revised Church of The Living God	5-Apr-88
211.	Alpha Church of God	7-Apr-88
212.	Apostolic Faith Church of God	20-Apr-88
213.	Open Bible Wesleyan Interdenominational Church	26-Apr-88
214.	Calvary Evangelistic Church of God	25-May-88
215.	Mount Bethel Baptist Church	25-May-88
216.	United Pentecostal Christian Church of God	14-Jun-88
217.	The Revival Hour Mission	5-Jul-88
218.	Faith Assembly Ministries	21-Jul-88

219.	The Church Dayton Diamond Ridge	21-Jul-88
220.	United Missionary Church Institute of Christ (Jamaica)	22-Sep-88
221.	Heaven Bound Gospel Assembly	26-Sep-88
222.	Emanuel's Hope Baptist Church Incorporated & Restored P.C.O.G of Jamaica.	27-Sep-88
223.	All People Church of God In Christ	4-Oct-88
224.	Fishers Temple	24-Oct-88
225.	Faith Land New World Ministries	31-Oct-88
226.	Love and Faith World Outreach Ministries	14-Nov-88
227.	Bibleway Church of God in Christ Jesus New Deal	7-Dec-88
228.	Davidian Seventh Day Adventist Association	13-Dec-88
229.	Miracle Valley Apostolic Church	19-Jan-89
230.	Mount Zion Baptist Church	26-Jan-89
231.	The Restored Church of Jesus Christ	1-Feb-89
232.	The Church of Jesus Christ Pentecostal	22-Feb-89
233.	Lord of Lords Evan. Outreach Heal. Cen.	6-Mar-89
234.	Faith and Hope Pentecostal Apostolic Church of Jesus Christ	13-Mar-89
235.	The Sabbath Day Church of God	4-Apr-89
236.	Revival Independent Baptist Church	6-Apr-89
237.	Faith Fellowship Pentecostal Apostolic Church	7-Apr-89
238.	The Ole Country Church Calvary Gospel Assembly	8-Apr-89
239.	Covenant On The Rock Deliverance Ministries	10-Apr-89
240.	The Holy Ghost Church of God	12-Apr-89
241.	Calvary Church of God In Christ (Jamaica)	18-Apr-89
242.	The Association of Independent Baptist Churches	25-May-89
243.	Full Gospel Church in Christ	29-May-89
244.	Bethlehem Assembly Prayer House Church of God	19-Jun-89
245.	Elohim Church of Prayer Jamaica	11-Jul-89
246.	Mandeville Meetings Rooms Trust Company	13-Jul-89
247.	Triumphant Church of Jesus Christ Apostolic	13-Jul-89
248.	Faith Fellowship Ministries World Outreach Center	25-Aug-89
249.	International Apostolic Ministries	28-Aug-89
250.	Pentecost - The Lighthouse Apostolic	29-Aug-89
251.	Mount Calvary United Zion Revival Church of Christ	31-Aug-89
252.	The Tree of Life Church of God	15-Sep-89
253.	United Emanuel Holiness Churches of the Apostolic Faith of Jamaica	2-Oct-89
254.	Victory Temple	23-Oct-89

CHURCH NAME	Incorporation date
255. The Hope Fellowship	27-Oct-89
256. Gospel Guide Church of God	9-Nov-89
257. Jerusalem Church of God 7th Day (Jamaica)	20-Nov-89
258. Church Of God Universal (Jamaica)	4-Dec-89
259. Good News Ministries	6-Dec-89
260. The Newness of Life Church of God	11-Dec-89
261. First Tabernacle Church of Jesus Christ Apostolic	12-Dec-89
262. The Mount Olivet Church of Christ Apostolic	5-Jan-90
263. Carmel New Testament Church of Our Lord	10-Jan-90
264. The Mount Zion Apostolic Church of Jamaica	1-Feb-90
265. Little Shiloh Apostolic Gospel Temple	2-Feb-90
266. Church Of God World-Wide Mission (Pentecostal)	8-Feb-90
267. Faithful Gospel Church of God	13-Feb-90
268. One Way Apostolic Church Association	14-Feb-90
269. Kingston Church of Christ	15-Feb-90
270. The Bethel Born Again Church of Jesus Christ	22-Feb-90
271. The Reform United Church of God	6-Mar-90
272. The Search of Life Church of God	9-Apr-90
273. The National Full Gospel Missionary Baptist Fellowship Jamaica and America	12-Apr-90
274. United Pentecostal Bethlehem Assembly Of Jesus	3-May-90
275. The Wayside Bethany Assembly Church	9-May-90
276. Bible Way Apostolic Church	14-May-90
277. Faith Claim Ministries	24-May-90
278. The Living Word Ministries Church	4-Jun-90
279. Faith Bible Church	10-Jul-90
280. Christian Service International	31-Jul-90
281. United Purchased Church of God Deliverance Centre	16-Aug-90
282. The Baptist Pentecostal Church of God	31-Aug-90
283. The Apostolic Church of Jesus Christ	20-Sep-90
284. Ark of Salvation Apostolic Church of God	25-Sep-90
285. Life Faith Ministries International	4-Oct-90
286. Cathedral Church of The Living God	1-Nov-90
287. Revival Temple of Jamaica	6-Nov-90
288. Goodness Out Reach Ministry	21-Nov-90
289. Morant Bay Church of Christ	15-Jan-91
290. Bethel Christian Retreat	21-Jan-91
291. Living Faith Bible Church	6-Feb-91
292. The True Prayer Line Church of God	4-Mar-91

CHURCH NAME	Incorporation date
293. National Baptist Spiritual Church of God	10-Apr-91
294. Assemblies of Holiness	11-Apr-91
295. Calvary Revival Assembly	22-Apr-91
296. Calvary Church of God	3-May-91
297. Heavenly Healing Church of Christ Bible Way	16-May-91
298. The Assembly Church of God	30-May-91
299. Holy Trinity Spiritual Baptist Church	5-Jun-91
300. The Miracle Church of God	4-Jul-91
301. The New Life Tabernacle (BW)	6-Aug-91
302. Holiness United Pentecostal Church	14-Aug-91
303. Triumphant Deliverance Full Gospel Assembly	14-Aug-91
304. Beulah Church of Jesus Christ - Apostolic	27-Aug-91
305. The Rehoboth Apostolic Church	4-Sep-91
306. The Holy Ghost Assembly Church of God	12-Sep-91
307. The World Baptist Fellowship of the West Indies	19-Sep-91
308. Church of Jesus Christ Blessing Plan Ministry	26-Sep-91
309. Harvest Time Church of God	26-Sep-91
310. Church of God of The First Born (Seventh Day)	28-Oct-91
311. Bread of Life Ministries	11-Dec-91
312. The Royal Flat Community Faith Church	16-Dec-91
313. True Tabernacle Church of Jesus Christ Apostolic	2-Jun-92
314. Bethel Bible Way Church of our Lord Jesus Christ	7-Jun-92
315. Apostolic Brethren of Christ Zion Sabbath Church	17-Sep-92
316. Carmel Fellowship Spiritual Church	17-Sep-92
317. Mount Zion Revival Holy Church of Jamaica	29-Oct-92
318. Mount Carmel Apostolic Faith In Jesus Christ	19-Nov-92
319. Pilgrim Holiness Rescue Mission	7-Dec-92
320. Homestead Fellowship Church of God	21-Dec-92
321. Christian Out Reach Missionary Evangelism	6-Jan-93
322. Soul Seekers Gospel Team of Jamaica	8-Jan-93
323. National Baptist Full Gospel Church	8-Feb-93
324. Tri - Parish Prayer Rooms Ministries	23-Feb-93
325. Rae Town New Testament Church of God	25-Feb-93
326. Saint Michael's Zion Spiritual Church	1-Mar-93
327. The O/N Comm. Keep of the Church of the Living God	2-Mar-93
328. Seventh Day Church of God Inter Ministries	24-Mar-93
329. Montego Bay Church of Christ	31-Mar-93
330. The New Temple Church of God	15-Apr-93
331. Open Heart Ministries	28-Apr-93

CHURCH NAME	Incorporation date
332. The New Faith True Church of God	28-Apr-93
333. The Spiritual Church of Jesus Christ	2-Jul-93
334. Kingston Family Church	26-Jul-93
335. Victory Faith Tabernacle Church of God	5-Aug-93
336. Mt Bethel Zion Apostolic Church of Christ Assembly	18-Aug-93
337. Trinity Church of God in Christ	23-Aug-93
338. Faith Temple Pentecostal Assemblies	2-Sep-93
339. The Lord Our Righteousness Church of God	10-Sep-93
340. Good Look Church of God Ministries	14-Sep-93
341. Light House Assembly	14-Sep-93
342. Power Ministry	14-Sep-93
343. Angels of God Zion Sabbath Hall	16-Sep-93
344. New Testament Assembly in Christ	16-Sep-93
345. Mount Everest Holiness Church of God	27-Sep-93
346. Gethsemane Church of God in Christ	4-Oct-93
347. Jamaica Come Back To God Evangelistic Outreach Ministry	22-Oct-93
348. The Church of Faith Gospel (Foundation) Church of Jamaica	22-Oct-93
349. Global Church of Mt Ephraim True Sabbath Observers	26-Oct-93
350. Calvary's Fountain Full Gospel Church of God	2-Nov-93
351. Mount Zion Holy Ghost Church of God	2-Nov-93
352. Grove Place Mount Zion Revival Church Company	5-Nov-93
353. Equator Faith Mission Church of God Association	8-Nov-93
354. The Church of Haile Selassie	12-Nov-93
355. Servant's Heart Ministry	14-Nov-93
356. The Straight Gate Church of Jesus Christ (Apostolic)	16-Nov-93
357. The Beulah Born Again Apostolic Church of Jesus Christ	18-Nov-93
358. Jamaica Church of the Living God	25-Nov-93
359. Yahvah - Pillar and Ground of Truth	30-Nov-93
360. Church of Jesus Christ United Faith Apostolic	2-Dec-93
361. Zion Sacred Heart of Christ Sabbath Church	6-Dec-93
362. Spanish Town Light House Assembly	7-Dec-93
363. United Lifeline Deliverance Church of God	7-Dec-93
364. Caribbean Praise Network	8-Dec-93
365. Christian Benevolent Outreach, International	15-Dec-93
366. Upper Room Community Church	16-Dec-93

367. New Generation Ministries	13-Jan-94
368. Word Power Ministries International	14-Jan-94
369. Meadowbrook United Church Trust	17-Jan-94
370. Unique Christian Fellowship	7-Feb-94
371. The Church of God (Jamaican Assembles)	8-Feb-94
372. The Heat Gospel Explorers Ministries	15-Feb-94
373. Good News Release Centre of the Prophetic Church of God	21-Feb-94
374. St James Apostolic United Zion Church	23-Feb-94
375. Jesus Inner -Healing Ministries Foundation	28-Feb-94
376. World of Faith Ministries Ocho Rios	8-Mar-94
377. Deliverance Church of God of Jamaica	18-Mar-94
378. Freedom Hall Church of God	24-Mar-94
379. Caribbean Apostolic Fellowship Association	13-May-94
380. Assemblies of Faith Ministries	3-Jun-94
381. Church of God of the Apostolic Faith	7-Jun-94
382. Zion Holiness Church of God	10-Jun-94
383. Star of Mount Zion Church of God	16-Jun-94
384. First Century Apostolic Church	6-Jul-94
385. Zion Deliverance Center	7-Jul-94
386. Church of God Rock of Holiness Foundation	8-Jul-94
387. Church of God (Universal)	20-Jul-94
388. Full Gospel Opendoor Assembly	8-Aug-94
389. New Triumphant Pentecostal Church of God	10-Aug-94
390. Gethsemane Baptist Church	15-Aug-94
391. Triumphant Tabernacle of Praise	22-Aug-94
392. Christian Community Church, St Mary	7-Sep-94
393. The Fire Baptized Holiness Church of God of the Americas	5-Oct-94
394. Mount Zion Healing Church of Christ	15-Dec-94
395. World Christian Fellowship and Outreach Ministries	12-Jan-95
396. Independent Baptist Church Planters	24-Jan-95
397. Miracle Mercy Mission Gospel Church	3-Feb-95
398. The Door Christian Fellowship Church	13-Feb-95
399. Kingsland Congregation of Jehovah's Witnesses	13-Mar-95
400. Shekinah Ministries	19-Mar-95
401. Redeemed United Holy Church Of God	29-Mar-95
402. New Gospel Way S.D. Church of God	28-Apr-95
403. One Accord Church of God	11-May-95

CHURCH NAME	Incorporation date
404. Restoration Christian Assembly Ministries	2-Jun-95
405. The Soul Winning Ministry of Jamaica	2-Jun-95
406. Greater Grace Temple Shiloh Apostolic Church	20-Jun-95
407. Fellowship Spiritual Apostolic Church	5-Jul-95
408. Harvest Temple ' Apostolic'	21-Jul-95
409. The Universal Centre of Truth for Better Living	14-Sep-95
410. Faith Miracle Life Fellowship Spiritual Church	15-Sep-95
411. Faith and Deliverance Outreach Ministry	17-Oct-95
412. Harvest Ministries	25-Oct-95
413. Miracle Faith Ministry of King	2-Nov-95
414. Church of Jesus Christ According to Acts 2:38	13-Nov-95
415. Sacred Heart Spiritual Church of Jesus Christ	30-Nov-95
416. Zion International Evangelism Crusades	1-Dec-95
417. Miracle Tabernacle Church of God	19-Dec-95
418. Caribbean Deeper Christian Life Fellowship	10-Jan-96
419. Jerusalem St Michael's Spiritual Zion Church	1-Feb-96
420. Franciscan Ministries	7-Feb-96
421. The Lighthouse Evangelistic Association of Jamaica	13-Feb-96
422. Church of The Living Light	22-Feb-96
423. Pentecost Church of Jamaica of Worldwide Missionary Movement	1-Mar-96
424. All Jesus Apostolic Nations Fellowship	20-Mar-96
425. Mount Olivet Open Bible Fellowship Spiritual Church Company	27-Mar-96
426. Power in the Word Church of God International	16-Apr-96
427. Holiness Christian Fellowship	30-Apr-96
428. Revival Fellowship Baptist Church	2-May-96
429. Evangelistic Outreach Ministry	13-May-96
430. Power of Hope Deliverance Ministry	15-May-96
431. The New United Bible Way Church of God	27-May-96
432. The House of Faith Spiritual Baptist Church	29-May-96
433. Mount Nazareth Spiritual Healing Temple	31-May-96
434. The Church of the Lord Jesus - Faith of the Apostles - Jamaica	24-Jun-96
435. Jamaica Light And Life Full Gospel Fellowship Church	26-Jun-96
436. Power Line Evangelistic Ministry	9-Jul-96
437. God Is Love - Pentecostal Church	18-Jul-96

CHURCH NAME	Incorporation date
438. Cornerstone Fellowship	6-Aug-96
439. The Apostolic Worship Centre Ministries	12-Aug-96
440. Faith Produces Miracle Ministry	23-Aug-96
441. Ebenezer Pentecostal Church	26-Aug-96
442. Portmore Apostolic Church	2-Sep-96
443. The Latterrain Outreach Ministry	3-Sep-96
444. Faith Fellowship Missionary Zion Church	20-Sep-96
445. The Brotherhood of The Cross and Star	26-Sep-96
446. Lutheran Ministries In Jamaica	9-Oct-96
447. Apostolic Healing Temple	24-Oct-96
448. New Creation Baptist Church	1-Nov-96
449. Full-Gospel Faith Ministries	13-Nov-96
450. Mt. Zion Seventh Day Church of God	15-Nov-96
451. The Universal Church of The Kingdom of God	13-Dec-96
452. Grace Church of Our Lord Jesus Christ Apostolic	18-Dec-96
453. United Fellowship Ministry	9-Jan-97
454. Foursquare Christian Fellowship	28-Jan-97
455. The Jamaica First Born Church of God	30-Jan-97
456. Togetherness Church of God	20-Feb-97
457. Hosanna Ministries Jamaica	10-Mar-97
458. Faith Triumphant Church of God	7-Apr-97
459. Apostolic Spiritual Church of God	2-May-97
460. The Voice of The Redeem Spiritual Church	9-May-97
461. Island Missionary Society	19-May-97
462. Resurrection Lighthouse Full Gospel Pentecostal Tabernacle	1-Jul-97
463. The Spaldings Church	21-Jul-97
464. He Restoreth My Soul Ministries	22-Aug-97
465. Church of God World Fellowship	28-Aug-97
466. Compassion Evangelistic Association Church of God	29-Aug-97
467. Old Timey Missionary Baptists Church	4-Sep-97
468. House of Mount Zion Walk In The Light	8-Sep-97
469. Christian Church of Jesus Christ The Supreme	11-Sep-97
470. Fairfield Road Church of Jesus Christ Ministry	25-Sep-97
471. Praise Tabernacle	25-Sep-97
472. Seventh Day Church of God (Reformed)	29-Sep-97
473. Council of International Fellowship (C.I.F.) Jamaica	9-Oct-97
474. Jerusalem House of Prayer (The Refuge Center)	13-Nov-97
475. Christian Community of The Holy Spirit	18-Nov-97

CHURCH NAME	Incorporation date
476. Purchase Redemption Church of God	21-Nov-97
477. Innercity for Christ Ministries	26-Nov-97
478. The Good Samaritan	27-Nov-97
479. Faith Fullgospel Deliverance Church of God	28-Nov-97
480. The Ethiopian Believers Assembly Jamaica	9-Dec-97
481. Mount Zion Revival Church of God	10-Dec-97
482. Berean Church of God International	11-Dec-97
483. Tree of Life Pentecostal Church of God	15-Jan-98
484. The True Church of Jesus Christ	22-Jan-98
485. United Way Church of God	22-Jan-98
486. Faith Healing and Deliverance Inspired Ministries	27-Jan-98
487. Mount Sinai Spiritual Church of God	13-Feb-98
488. Faith Bible Baptist Church	5-Mar-98
489. Little Shiloh Pentecostal Tabernacle	6-Mar-98
490. Sons of God in Christ Jesus Apostolic	10-Mar-98
491. The New Creation Church of God	10-Mar-98
492. Redeemed Pilgrims Ministry (Jamaica)	13-Mar-98
493. Church of God Faith Assemblies	16-Mar-98
494. Faith and Deliverance Ministries International	27-Mar-98
495. Temple of Light Church of God	4-May-98
496. Nehemiah International Foundation	5-May-98
497. Church of the Living Creator, The Holy One of Israel	6-May-98
498. Oneness Jesus Church Ministries	8-May-98
499. The Church in Communities (Itinerant)	13-May-98
500. The Redeemed Christian Church of God	19-May-98
501. Restoration of Life Mission in Christ	1-Jun-98
502. Little Zion Faith Healing Temple	3-Jun-98
503. The New Church of God	15-Jun-98
504. The Resurrected Church of God	25-Jun-98
505. Corner Stone Apostolic Church	26-Jun-98
506. Sandy Bay Baptist Church	1-Jul-98
507. Blessing and Deliverance Ministries	6-Jul-98
508. Holiness Apostolic Church	13-Jul-98
509. Church of Christ Jamaica Evangelism Projects	21-Jul-98
510. Henry Fernandez Ministries-Plantation Worship Centre	22-Jul-98
511. The Church of God Body of Christ (Jamaica) Conference	28-Jul-98
512. Love Light Zion Church	30-Jul-98

CHURCH NAME	Incorporation date
513. Norbrook River of Life Tabernacle	7-Aug-98
514. Emmanuel Baptist Church	11-Aug-98
515. Ten Commandments Church of God	18-Aug-98
516. Mandeville Family Church and Ministries	6-Oct-98
517. The Ethiopian Coptic Rite Church	27-Oct-98
518. The Church of Jesus Christ of Jamaica Healing Mission	20-Nov-98
519. The Rock Ministries United	22-Dec-98
520. Caribbean Conference of the Seventh-Day Christians	7-Jan-99
521. Ancient Restorers Apostolic Church of Jesus Christ	8-Jan-99
522. The Valencia Church of Jesus Christ	21-Jan-99
523. The Brethren United Zion Christ Church	25-Jan-99
524. International Worship Centre & Faith Ministries	26-Jan-99
525. New Covenant Worship Center	3-Feb-99
526. Deliverance Temple Apostolic Church	9-Feb-99
527. Faith and Mission Outreach Ministry	10-Feb-99
528. Miracle Temple Ministries	18-Feb-99
529. Jamaica Outreach Ministries	19-Feb-99
530. Global Missions	3-Mar-99
531. Grange Hill Church of Christ	4-Mar-99
532. Highgate Church of Christ	4-Mar-99
533. Port Maria Church of Christ	4-Mar-99
534. St Ann's Bay Church of Christ	4-Mar-99
535. Victory Temple Apostolic Church	15-Mar-99
536. The Miracle Prayer Centre	13-Apr-99
537. Truth & Light Church of Y'shua-Jesus Christ Apostolic	15-Apr-99
538. River of Life Tabernacle-Jamaica	26-Apr-99
539. Seven Seals Church of God	6-May-99
540. Fresh Fire Ministries International	11-May-99
541. In Touch Gospel Church of God	12-May-99
542. True Missionary Church of God Ministries	14-May-99
543. Last Days Church of God	27-May-99
544. New Life Ministries of Jamaica	25-Jun-99
545. Overcomers Christian International	13-Jul-99
546. Members In Christ Assemblies	26-Jul-99
547. Ebenezer International Development Organization	8-Nov-99

Source: *Registrar of Companies 2001 List of Churches*

Appendix II: Denominations incorporated by Parliament

Year	Denomination
1884	Moravian Church; United Presbyterians+
1917	AME Zion Church
1929	Society of Jesuits in Jamaica*
1949	Church of God and Saints of Christ
	New Testament Church of God
	Pilgrim Holiness Church
	Holiness Christian Church
	Missionary Bands of The World
	United Pentecostal Church of Jamaica
	Church of God Holiness
1954	Emanuel Apostle United Church of Christ
	Sisters of Mercy of Jamaica, British West Indies
	Holiness Church
	Jamaica Faith Mission
	Church of God in Christ Jesus Apostolic
1956	Missionary Churches Association in Jamaica
	Bible Truth Church of God
1957	Open Bible Standard Churches
	The African Reform Church of God in Christ
1958	Good Tidings Mennonite Church
1960	Pentecostal Assemblies of Jamaica
	Gospel Foundation Church of Jamaica
1964	Jamaica Presbyterian Corporation+
	Baptist Mid-Missions In Jamaica
	Church of God of Prophecy of Jamaica
1969	African Methodist Episcopal Church
	Jamaica Baptist Union
1970	Roman Catholic Archbishop of Kingston and the Roman Catholic Bishop of Montego Bay
1973	Unity Church of Jamaica
	Church of God in Christ
	Christadelphia Bible Mission
	Saint Andrew Apostolic Temple
	Church of the First Born
	Rainbow Healing Temple
	New Testament Church of God

Year	Denomination
	Christ Gospel Church International (Jamaica) Incorporation
1978	Glad Tidings Church of the First Born
	Ethiopian Orthodox Church in Jamaica
	Holy Temple Church of The Lord Jesus Christ
1980	Jamaica Bible Church
	Bethel Church of God and Saints of Christ
1988	House of God Church
	Church of Jesus Christ of Latter Day Saints
	Church of the United Brethren in Christ (Jamaica Conference)
	Deliverance Evangelistic Association
	Jamaica Council Church of God Seventh-Day
	Passionist Community of Jamaica
	Mount Zion Church of God
	Assembly of Yahweh
1992	Full Gospel Fellowship Church of Lord Jesus Christ
	Church of Haile Selaisse 1
	Christian Fellowship World Outreach
	The United Church in Jamaica and the Cayman Islands+
	Church of Christ Jamaica
	United Holy Revival Church of Jamaica
	West Indies Union Conference (Jamaica), Corporation of Seventh Day Adventists
1995	New Testament Church of Christ the Redeemer
	The Sons & Daughters United Church of God
	The Church of Living God
1996	Society of Jesus*
	Lutheran Ministries in Jamaica

Same organisation, just a name change
+These are denominations that have merged

Source: *House of Parliament 'Church Bills' 1884-1995 & Other Bills*

Appendix III: List of Roman Catholic Training Centres

Kingston & St Andrew

Alpha Boys' School
Christ the King Evening Education Institute
Gordon Town Training Centre
Laws Street Trade Training Centre
Our Lady of the Angels Housecraft Training Institute
Stella Maris Training Centre
St Anne's Community Centre of Concern in Western Kingston
St Margaret's Human Resource Centre
St Patrick's Human Resource Centre
St Pius X Skills Training Centre
St Theresa's Adult Outreach Centre

St Catherine

Above Rocks Vocational Training Centre
Above Rocks Pre-Vocational School
Above Rocks Special School

Manchester

Holy Cross Arts & Craft
Mandeville Catholic College (Adult)
Our Lady of the Assumption Arts & Craft
St John Bosco Building Training
St John Bosco Butcher School
St John Bosco Catering School

Source: *Catholic Directory 1997-1999*

Appendix IV: Jamaica Baptist Union Medical & Dental Clinics

MEDICAL

DENTAL

Kingston & St Andrew
  Barbican Baptist
  Bethel Baptist
  East Queen Street Baptist
  Hanover Street Baptist
  Tarrant Baptist

St Ann
  Higgins Land Baptist
  Ocho Rios Baptist

St Catherine
  Edgewater Baptist
  Gregory Park Baptist
  Bethel, Bog Walk Baptist
  Point Hill Baptist

Manchester
  Mandeville Baptist
  New Green Baptist

St James
  Calvary Baptist

Clarendon
  Grace Baptist

Trelawny
  Kettering Baptist

St Elizabeth
  Burn Savannah Baptist

Kingston & St Andrew
  Boulevard Baptist
  East Queen Street Baptist

Manchester
  Mandeville Baptist

Source: *Directory of Social Services of the Churches of the Jamaica Baptist Union*

Appendix V: The Denominations that Opposed the Lottery

1. Anglican
2. Roman Catholic
3. Methodist
4. Jamaica Baptist Union
5. United Church of Jamaica
6. The Moravian Church in Jamaica
7. The Disciples of Christ
8. Salvation Army
9. Society of Friends
10. African Methodist Episcopal
11. The Church of God in Jamaica
12. Jamaica Association of Evangelicals
13. Jamaica Evangelistic Mission
14. Associated Gospel Assemblies
15. Missionary Church Association
16. Church of the First Born
17. United Brethren in Christ
18. Open Bible Standard
19. Jamaica Theological Seminary
20. Jamaica Bible School
21. Church of God Holiness

Source: *Daily Gleaner July 7, 1968*

Appendix VI: Roman Catholic Preparatory Schools (1999)

Archdiocese of Kingston

Alvernia
Holy Childhood
Holy Rosary
Immaculate Conception
Our Lady of the Angels
Msgr. Colin Bryan
Stella Maris
St John the Baptist
Sts Peter & Paul
St Theresa's
St Catherine
St Helen's

Diocese of Montego Bay

Mt Alvernia
Columbus

Vicariate of Mandeville

Mount St Joseph
Sacred Heart Academy
St John Bosco
St Robert Bellarmine
St Thomas More

Source: *Catholic Directory 1997-1999*

Appendix VII: Distribution of Church Buildings
According to Denomination

Denomination	Number
New Testament Church of God	350
Adventist	320
Baptist	300
Anglican	298
Church of God of Prophecy	280
Catholic	198
Salvation Army	183
Methodist	172
United Church	146
Church of God	107
Pentecostal	100
Brethren	82
Assemblies of God	72
City Mission	70
Moravian	51
Open Bible	45
Missionary	42
Church of First Born	41
Deliverance Centre	26
Total	2,883

Source: *The New Testament Church of God 75th Anniversary Supplement 2000, Denominational Records & Personal Communication*

BIBLIOGRAPHY

PRIMARY SOURCES

Jamaica Archives
PP, 1866, (3683) XXX, Report of the Jamaica Royal Commission.
PP, 1866, (3683-1), XXX1, Report of the Jamaica Royal Commission, Part 11, Minutes of Evidence and Appendix.

SECONDARY SOURCES

Journals & Papers

Abstract of Statistics, No. 18. December 1958, Department of Statistics, Jamaica, W.I. (Government Printers: Kingston, 1959).

Abstract of Statistics, No. 19. December 1959, Department of Statistics, Jamaica, W.I. (Government Printers: Kingston, 1960).

Bank of Jamaica Annual Report (2000) Kingston.

Catholic Directory 1997-1999.

Directory of Educational Institutions 2000-2001. Planning and Development Division, Ministry of Education and Culture, Kingston.

ECLOF Annual Report 1999. Geneva.

Eighth Census of Jamaica and its Dependencies 1943 Population, Housing and Agriculture (National Library).

Jamaican Historical Society Bulletin Vol. 11 No. 6 October 2000.

Jamaica National Directors' Report & Financial Statement 2000.

Jamaica Survey of Living Conditions 1999 A Joint Publication of the Planning Institute of Jamaica and The Statistical Institute of Jamaica August 2000,

Police Statistics Department Report 2001.

The Wortley Home 1918-2000 (Kingston: Maurice Hill, 2001).

1998 Pocketbook of Statistics (Kingston: Statistical Institute of Jamaica, 1998).

2000 Demographic Statistics (Kingston: Statistical Institute of Jamaica, 2000).

Newspapers (National Library & Gleaner Library)

a) Articles

Ian Boyne, 'Outstanding Church Leaders', Jamaica 25 Supplement, *The Gleaner*, August 1, 1987, pp 56-57.

Ingrid Brown, 'Stagnant Gospel?', *The Star*, January 26, 2000, p.11.

Michael Burke, 'Don't Knock Celibacy', *The Jamaica Observer*, July 27, 2000, p.6.

Devon Dick, 'Scratch and Lose', *The Jamaica Herald*, November 29, 1992, p.5A

Devon Dick, 'The Church in this Century (Part I)', *The Gleaner*, December 27, 1999, pA14

Devon Dick, 'The Church in this Century (Part II)', *The Gleaner*, December 28, 1999, pD4

Peter Espeut, 'Marginalising Males', *The Gleaner*, January 26, 2000, p. A4.

Ernle Gordon, 'The Nation's Oldest Church Buildings', *The Gleaner*, January 25, 2000, p. A5.

Billy Hall, 'Trends in the Jamaican Church', Jamaica 25 Supplement, *The Gleaner*, August 1, 1987, pp 54-55.

Michele Johnson, 'A Century of Murder in Jamaica, 1880-1980', *Jamaica Journal*, Vol. 20, no. II. pp. 34-40

Cecilia Legister, 'Dale Flynn...Putting Life into Jamaican Gospel', *The Jamaica Observer*, June 19, 2000, p. 29.

Una Marson, 'A Better Way', *The Gleaner*, October 25, 1961.

Errol Miller, 'The Green Paper and the Delinquent State', *The Gleaner*, February 17, 2000, p. A4.

Winston Ridgard, 'Defending Love 101 and Love TV', *The Jamaica Observer*, November 3, 2001, p.7.

Dr Horace Russell, 'The Church in Jamaica An Overview of the Past 25 Years', Jamaica 25 Supplement, *The Gleaner*, August 1, 1987, pp 50-52.

Joy Scott, 'The Oldest British Cathedral', *Skywritings*, no. 40 April 1984, p. 7.

Phyllis Thomas, 'Methodist Church Marks Years in Jamaica', *The Star*, April 11, 1988, p. 10.

Ralph Thompson, 'Wanted: A New Vision for Education', *The Gleaner*, November 18, 2001, p. G1.

Michael Witter, 'Exchange Rate Policy in Jamaica: A Critical Assessment', *Social and Economic Studies*, vol. 33, December 1983.

b) Newspaper supplements and complete issues

Sunday Herald, January 30 - February 5, 1999, p. 20.

The Gleaner, 'Jamaica 25. Progress of a Nation, 1962-1987'. Independence Anniversary Supplement, August 1, 1987.

The Gleaner, 'Nation Prayer Breakfast Feature', January 20, 2000, p. A14.

The Sunday Gleaner, 'In Celebration of the 175th Anniversary of the Diocese 1825-2000 Advertisement', February 6, 2000, p. 14F.

The Gleaner, 'Victoria Mutual 122nd Anniversary Supplement', November 12, 2000.

The Gleaner, 'The New Testament Church of God 75th Anniversary Supplement', November 29, 2000.

The Gleaner, 'East Queen Street Baptist Church 200th Anniversary Feature', May 11, 2000, p. B10.

The Gleaner, 'Morant Bay High School 40th Anniversary Feature', April 10, 2001, pp. B5-B6.

The Gleaner, 'Northern Caribbean University Special Advertising Feature', May 15, 2001, pp. C5-C7.

The Gleaner, Outlook Magazine, '30th Anniversary Churches Co-operative Credit Union Ltd. Special Advertising Feature', November 25, 2001, pp 19-26.

The Star, 'The Jamaica Burial Scheme Society 100th Anniversary Feature', May 2, 2001, pp. 20-22.

The Weekend Observer, 'Clarendon College Homecoming 2000 a vision fulfilled', July 21, 2000, p. 23.

c) News Items/Stories

The Sunday Gleaner, June 24, 1956, 'Rennock Lodge Church-example of Unity.'

The Gleaner, October 18, 1956, 'We Methodists Will Take the lead - H. E.'

The Gleaner, January 24, 1957, 'Methodists Approve Loyalty Resolution'.

The Gleaner, February 9, 1958, 'Opening of Jamaica's First Mosque'.

The Gleaner, December 5, 1968, 'Clergymen Warned to be Careful What They Say in Sermons.'

The Gleaner, March 7, 1980, 'Crime and Violence in Jamaica: Causes and Solutions'.

The Gleaner, January 24, 2000, 'Methodist Annual Meeting on this Week'.

The Sunday Gleaner, April 30, 2000, 'Churches to Keep Tax-free Status'.

The Gleaner, May 18, 2000, 'Hotels Sense Casino Signal'.

The Gleaner, July 15, 2000, 'Reviewing Gospel Music with Sam Wisdom'.
The Sunday Gleaner, January 7, 2001, 'On the Role of the Church'.

The Jamaica Observer, December 27, 2001, 'A Boys' Home with Big Plans, But Little Funds'.

The Gleaner, February 6, 2002, 'Mount Olivet Boys' Home to get a Facelift'.

The Observer, April 1, 2002, 'Good Shephard Foundation Needs to Assist People with HIV/AIDS'.

BOOKS, THESES AND ARTICLES

Augier, F. R. & Shirley Gordon, (compilers), *Sources of West Indian History*. Kingston: Longman Caribbean, 1974.

Barclay, William, *New Testament Words*. London: SCM Press, 1964.

Barrett, David B., ed., *World Christian Encyclopedia*. Oxford: Oxford University Press, 1982.

Beckford, George L., *Persistent Poverty*. Morant Bay: Maroon Publishing House Ltd., 1988.

Beckles, Hilary and Verene Shepherd, eds., *Caribbean Freedom: Economy and Society from Emancipation to the Present*. Kingston: Ian Randle Publishers, 1996.

Brooks, A. A., *History of Bedwardism*. Kingston: P. A. Benjamin, 1909.

Brown, Georgia. 'Bishop Herro Blair: The Development of a Charismatic Leader in Contemporary Jamaican Society.' B.A. thesis, The University of the West Indies,1987.

Browne, Wintlett and Paulette Dunn, *Smith Primary Social Studies, Book 4A, The Parishes of Jamaica*. Kingston: Carlong Publishers (Caribbean) Ltd., 2000.

Buisseret, David, *Historic Architecture of the Caribbean*. London: Heinemann, 1980.

Carl Campbell, '*Abolition of Slavery & Education in Jamaica, 1834-64.*' Jamaican Historical Society Bulletin vol. 11, no. 7 (April 2001): 164-7.

Clarke, Colin, *Jamaica in Maps*. London: Hodder & Stoughton, 1974.

Davis, Edmund, *Theological Education in a Multi-Ethnic Society*. Zoetermeer: Boekencentrum Publishing House, 1998.

Dick, Devon, *Paul Bogle: Prophet without Honour*. Kingston: The University of the West Indies, M.A. thesis, 1997.

Chevannes, Barry, *Sexual Practices and Behaviour in Jamaica: A Review of the Literature*. Kingston: Aidscom, 1992.

Commissiong, Elaine, *The History of the Basic School Movement in Jamaica*. Netherlands: Bernard van Leer Foundation, 1999.

Cuthbert, Robert W. M., *Ecumenism and Development*. Bridgetown: Caribbean Contact Ltd., 1986

Davis, Edmund, *Men of Vision*. Kingston: Montrose Printery Ltd., 1981.

Davis, J. Merle, *The Church in the New Jamaica: A Study of the Economic and Social Basis of the Evangelical Church in Jamaica*. New York: Dept. of Social and Economic Research and Counsel, International Missionary Council, 1942.

Dexter, Noel, ed., *Caribbean School Hymnal*. Kingston: Longman, 1987.

Dookhan, Isaac, *A Pre-Emancipation History*. London: Longman, 1971.

Gordon, Shirley, *A Century of West Indian Education*. London: Longman, 1963.

Gordon, Shirley, *Our Cause For His Glory: Christianisation and Emancipation*. Kingston: The Press, 1998.

Grant, Dudley R.B., *A Better Educational Start For Jamaica's Children*. Kingston: UNICEF 1978.

Guy, Henry A. and Lavern Bailey, eds., *Women of Distinction in Jamaica*. Kingston: Caribbean Herald and associates, 1997

Hall, Douglas, *Free Jamaica, 1838-1865: An Economic History*. Barbados: Caribbean Universities Press, 1959.

Hastings, S. U. & B. L. Macleavy, *Seedtime and Harvest*. Bridgetown: Cedar Press, 1979.

Holt, Thomas C., *The Problem of Freedom: Race, Labor, and Politics in Jamaica and Britain, 1832-1938*. Kingston: Ian Randle Publishers, 1992.

Hutton, Clinton, 'Colour for Colour; Skin for Skin: The Ideological Foundations of post-slavery society, 1838-1865'. The Jamaica Case. PhD. Thesis, The University of the West, 1992.

Ingram, K. E. (ed.), *Libraries, Literacy and Learning*. Kingston: Jamaica Library Association, 1994.

Leo-Rhynie, Elsa, *The Jamaican Family*. Kingston: Grace Kennedy Lecture, 1993.

Lindo, Donald, *Time Tells Our Story*. Kingston: Ian Randle Publishers, 1994.

Long, L.J., *Ministry of Education Early Childhood Education Programme*. Kingston: Ministry of Education, March 1983.

Miller, Errol, *Jamaica in the 21st Century: Contending Choices*. Kingston: Grace, Kennedy Foundation, 2001.

Miller, Errol, *Education For All In The Caribbean In The 1990s*. Kingston: UNESCO, 2000.

Miller, Errol, *Marginalization of the Black Male: Insights from the Development of the Teaching Profession*. Kingston: Canoe Press, 1994.

Miller, Errol, *Jamaican Society and High Schooling*. Kingston: Institute of Social and Economic Research, 1990.

Moore, Brian & Swithin Wilmot, *Before and After 1865: Education, Politics and Regionalism in the Caribbean*. Kingston: Ian Randle Publishers, 1998.

Osborne, Francis J., *History of the Catholic Church in Jamaica*. London: Caribbean Universities Press, 1977.

Osborne, Francis J. and Godfrey Johnson, *Coastlands and Islands*. Kingston: UTCWI, 1972.

Patterson, Orlando, *Freedom: Freedom in the making of the Western Culture*. London: I.B.Tauris & Co. Ltd., 1991.

Patterson, Patricia & James Carnegie, *The People who came Book 2*. Trinidad and Tobago: Longman Caribbean, 1972.

Phillippo, J.M., *Jamaica, its Past and Present State*. London: Dawsons of Pall Mall, London, 1969.

Reid, Audley, *Community Formation*. Kingston: Canoe Press, 2000.

Revised Standard Version, *The Bible*. Great Britain: Collins Clear Type Press, 1975.

Robotham, Don, "The Notorious Riot". The Socio-economic and Political Bases of Paul Bogle's Revolt, Working paper 8. Jamaica: University of the West Indies, Institute of Social and Economical Research, 1981.

Russell, Horace O., *The Missionary Outreach of the West Indian Church*. New York: Peter Lang, 2000.

Sayles, Elsie, *CVSS-The First Fifty Years*. Kingston: Kingston Publishers, 1994.

Senior, Olive, *A-Z of Jamaican Heritage*. Kingston: Heinemann Educational Books (Caribbean) Ltd., 1983.

Shepherd, Verene, *Transients to Settlers: The Experience of Indians in Jamaica, 1845 - 1950*. Leeds: Peepal Tree, University of Warwick, 1994

Sherlock, Philip and Hazel Bennett, *The Story of the Jamaican People*. Kingston: Ian Randle Publishers, 1998.

Stewart, Robert, *Religion and Society in Post-Emancipation Jamaica*. Knoxville: The University of Tennessee Press, 1992.

Stone, Carl, *Class, State and Democracy in Jamaica*. Kingston: Blackett Publishers, 1985.

Sullivan, John Peter, *Twenty-One Years of Service: Jamaica's Credit Union Story*. Kingston: Jamaica Co-operative Credit Union League Ltd, 1963.

Taylor, Burchell, *Free For All? A Question Of Morality and Community*. Kingston: Grace Kennedy Lecture, 1997.

Taylor, Burchell, *Church Taking Sides*. Kingston: Bethel Baptist Church, 1995.

Taylor, Burchell, *Values and Attitudes-The Church's Responsibility*. Kingston: Bethel Baptist, 2000.

Underhill, E. B., *The West Indies: The Social and Religious Condition*. London: Jackson, Walford, and Hodder, 1862.

Underhill, E. B., *Life of James Mursell Phillippo, Missionary to Jamaica*. London: Yates and Alexander, 1881.

Walvin, James, *The Life and Times of Henry Clarke, 1828-1907*. Essex: Frank Cass & CO. Ltd., 1994.

West Indian Commission, Time for Action. Largo, Maryland: International Development Options & Mona: the Press, 1994.

Wright, Philip, *Knibb 'the Notorious': Slaves' Missionary 1803-1845*. London: Sidgwick & Jackson, 1973.

INDEX

Government Savings Bank; establishment of the, xvii

Government schools; elementary, 34-36

Government Training College; establishment of the, 30

Governor; powers under crown colony government of the, 61

Grace Thrillers; formation of the, 58

Grade Six Achievement Test (GSAT); introduction of the, 41

Grant, Sir John Peter; and development of state education, 35

Grant-in-aid Scheme; for secondary education, 39

Grey, Henry; and compensation for ex-slaves, xiv

Guys Hill; the church and community development in, 83

Hampton High School; establishment of, 49

Happy Grove High School, 39, 43

Harrison Memorial High School, 44

Hay, Canon John; missionary work of, 6

Health institutions see also clinics; established by the church, 24-25

Health services; provided by the church, 16, 104

Hill, Richard; victory at the polls, 59

Holy Childhood High School, 43

Holy Trinity High School, 43

Homes for the Aged; established by the church, 20-21

Homosexuality; the church and, 55

Hospitals; established by the church, 24-25

Housing; the church's role in the provision of, 13, 16, 78-79

Huggins, Lady Molly; and the mass wedding programme (1944); 53

Hurricane Gilbert; church aid to victims of, 26

Immaculate Conception High School; establishment of, 37, 38, 39, 43

Independence (1962), xv, 62; church's involvement in, xviii

Independent high schools; establishment of, 44

Independent Methodist Society; formation of the, 72

Infant schools, 45

Institute of Jamaica; establishment of the, xvii

Institutional development; church's role in, xvii, xix

Inter School Christian Fellowship, 56

International University of Biblical Studies; 32

Iona High School, 43

Jamaica Apostolic Bible Institute, 32

Jamaica Association of the Deaf; establishment of the, 19

Jamaica Baptist Union; clinics founded by the, 104

Jamaica Bible Institute of the Church of God, 32

Jamaica Bible School, 32

Jamaica Burial Scheme; establishment of the, 25

Jamaica Christian Council; establishment of the, 17

Jamaica College, 38; establishment of, 49

Jamaica Cooperative Credit Union League; establishment of the, 14

Jamaica Council of Churches (JCC); and gambling, 26-27; gospel crusades of the, 52-53; mediation in political violence, 64-66; role in the establishment of the UWI, 34

Jamaica its Past and Present State; description of free villages in, 8-9

Jamaica Labour Party (JLP); and gambling, 26

Jamaica Movement for the Advancement of Literacy (JAMAL); establishment and role of, 48-49

Jamaica National Building Society; development of the, 11-12

Jamaica Native Baptist Free Movement, 61

Jamaican Society and High Schooling, 37

Jamaica Theological Seminary, 32

Jamaica Union of Teachers; and empowerment of blacks, 61

Jamaica Youth for Christ Chorale; formation of the, 58

Jamaican Christian Council; formation of the, 66

Jamaican Church; charity provided by the, 15-22; definition of the use of the term, xiv-xv; and the development of building societies, 11-13; and the credit union movement, 13-15; and gambling, 26-28; and housing, 13; introduction and growth, 1-6; missionary work of the, 5-6; and the free village system, 7-11; and opportunities for nation building, xv-xvi; perceptions of state relationship with the, xv; taxation of the, 28

Jennings, Rev. Stephen; peace initiatives by, 65

Johnson, Rev. Pat, 76

Jones, Rev. Armon; chairman of the Methodist District (1930s), 61

Jordan, Edward; and formation of the Independent Methodist Society, 72

Judicial system; establishment of the, xvii

Junior secondary schools; establishment of, 40

Peace initiatives; by the church, 64-66
Peasantry; marriage rates among the, 53; political empowerment of the, 59-63; role of free villages on the development of the, 8-11
Pennock, Thomas; representation from Methodist church, 72
People's National Party (PNP); formation of the, 61; and gambling, 26-27
Philadelphia; free village, 10
Phillipo, Rev. James; challenge to the leadership of, 73; and the free village system, 8-9
Physically challenged; church centres for the, 18-20
Plantation society; socio-economic structure of, xiv
Political equality; Blacks and the struggle for, 59-67
Politics; role of the church in, 81-82
Port Maria High School, 44
Portland High School, 44
Porus; free village, 10
Preparatory schools; Roman Catholic, 106
Presbyterian Church; growth of the, 3; schools; 37; and teacher training, 30

Quaker schools, 43
Queens High School; establishment of the, 49

Racism see also Black racism; within the church, 72-73
Rastafarian Movement (1940s); and black dignity, 73
Rebellions; distinction between riots and, xvi; impact on national development, xvii, xvii; as opportunities for nation building by the church, xv
Religious media programmes; communicating family values through, 56-58
Riots see also rebellions; distinction between rebellion and, xvi; impact on national development, xvii, xviii; as opportunities for nation building by the church, xv
Riverside High School, 44
Rodney, Walter see Walter Rodney riots (1968)
Roman Catholic Church; black leadership in the, 73-74; and the credit union movement, 14; crusade against crime, 65; and gambling, 27; growth of the, 3; preparatory schools founded by the, 106; training centres founded by the, 103
Roman Catholic schools, 37, 43
Roots FM 96.1; establishment and role of, 58

Salem; free village, 10

Salvation Army; introduction of the, 1
Salvation Army Territorial Training College; 32
Sam Sharpe College; establishment of, 30
Savanna-La-Mar High School; 44
Secondary education; roles of church and the state in, 37-44
Seventh Day Adventist church; establishment of independent high schools by, 44; introduction of the, 1; and teacher training, 30
Sexuality; the church and, 54
Sexually Transmitted Diseases (STDs); the church and the fight against, 54
Shelters for the destitute; established by the church, 22
Sherlock, Rev. Hugh; missionary work of, 5
Sherlock, Sir Phillip; and the National Day of Prayer, 65
Shortwood Training College; establishment of, 30
Simpson, Rev. Herbert; missionary work of, 6
Slaves see freed slaves
Sligoville; free village, 8, 10
Smith, Rev. Ashley; religious advisor to Prime Minister Michael Manley, 62
Social Development Commission (SDC), 2
Social mobility; education as a strategy for, 50
Social stability; role of free villages in providing blacks with, 9-10
Social structure; of plantation society, xiv
Society of Friends; introduction of the, 1
Sodality Credit Union; establishment of the, 13
Spence, Rev. Herman; first black pastor of St Andrew Parish Church, 73
St Andrew High School, 39, 43
St Ann Building Society; establishment of the, 11
St Anne's High School, 43
St Ann's Bay High School, 44
St Catherine High School, 43
St Elizabeth Cooperative Credit Union; establishment of the, 14
St Georges College, 43; establishment of, 37, 38, 39
St Helena's, 39
St Hilda's High School, 38, 39, 43
St Hugh's High School, 39, 43
St Jago High School, 43
St Joseph's Teachers College; establishment of, 30
St Mary Building Society; establishment of the, 11-12
St Mary's High School, 43
Structural adjustment; consequences of, xvii
Sturge Town; free village, 10